SPENSER AND IRELAND

An Interdisciplinary Perspective

D1615670

Spenser and Ireland

An Interdisciplinary Perspective

edited by
PATRICIA COUGHLAN

with an introduction by
NICHOLAS CANNY

Cork University Press
1989

First published in 1989 by
Cork University Press, University College, Cork

British Library Cataloguing in Publication Data

Spenser and Ireland: an interdisciplinary perspective.
1. Poetry in English. Spenser, Edmund *1552?-1599*
I. Coughlan, Patricia
821.'3

ISBN 0-902561-55-3

Grant-aided by the National University of Ireland

Printed and typeset in Ireland by
Leinster Leader Ltd., Naas, Co. Kildare.

Contents

Note on Contributors

Ciaran Brady lectures in history at Trinity College, Dublin. He was co-editor, with Raymond Gillespie, of *Natives and Newcomers: Essays on the Making of Irish Colonial Society 1534-1641* (1986). He has published several essays in scholarly journals on various aspects of sixteenth-century Ireland.

Nicholas Canny is professor of modern history at University College, Galway. His principal publications are *The Elizabethan Conquest of Ireland* (1976) and *Ireland in the Atlantic World 1560-1800* (1988). He was co-editor, with Anthony Pagden, of *Colonial Identity in the Atlantic World 1500-1800* (1987).

Patricia Coughlan lectures in English at University College, Cork. She has published several articles on seventeenth-century English representations of Ireland, and has also contributed to various collections of criticism on later Anglo-Irish literature.

Anne Fogarty lectures in English at University College, Cork. She is currently completing a Ph.D. thesis on Spenser, and is the author of a forthcoming article on Sir John Davies.

Richard A. McCabe lectures in English Literature at Trinity College, Dublin. His publications include *Joseph Hall: A Study in Satire and Meditation* (1982), *The Pillars of Eternity: Time and Providence in "The Faerie Queene"* (1989), and numerous contributions to scholarly journals. scholarly journals.

Editor's Preface

This collection has its origins in a seminar which I organized in November 1985 under the auspices of the Medieval and Renaissance Society of University College, Cork, as an informal part of the commemoration of the eight hundredth anniversary of Cork's city charter. I should like to thank the students who then formed the committee of the society for their work in organizing the seminar, and the contributors. Thanks are also due to Tom Dunne of the Irish History Department, who first suggested the publication of the proceedings, and has provided useful advice along the way, to Anne Fogarty, who assisted greatly with the editing, and to Trevor Joyce who was the source of much encouragement. I am grateful to the Publications Committee of the National University of Ireland for a grant in aid of publication, and to Cork University Press and its executive secretary, Mr. Donal Counihan.

A Note on Texts

The editions of Spenser used throughout this book are, for the poetry: J. C. Smith and E. de Selincourt, ed., *Spenser: Poetical Works* (Oxford, 1912), and for the prose: W. L. Renwick, ed., *A View of the Present State of Ireland* (Oxford, 1970).

Introduction:
Spenser and the Reform of Ireland

NICHOLAS CANNY

It is appropriate that a collection of essays devoted to the subject of Spenser and Ireland should be published by Cork University Press. This is so first because Spenser's Irish experience was essentially a Munster or even a Cork one, and also because it was this same press which in 1928 drew international scholarly attention to the impact of his travails in Ireland upon the writings of Edmund Spenser when it published Pauline Henley's book *Spenser in Ireland*.[1]

The extent to which the subject has developed over the past sixty years becomes immediately apparent when the concerns of Pauline Henley in that path-breaking book are compared with the tone and thrust of the essays in the present collection. What was previously of interest only to students of literature is now proving of equal interest to historians, and there is also some evidence that the writings of Edmund Spenser warrant the attention of students of social and political theory.[2] No longer is it accepted, as it was in 1928, that Spenser's creative and polemical writings can be treated as discrete entities. Instead the several authors in this collection (as indeed elsewhere) make frequent references to *The Faerie Queene* when seeking to elucidate passages of *A View of the Present State of Ireland*, while the arguments expounded in the *View* are frequently employed to shed light on the message that Spenser was attempting to convey in his poetry. The fact that historians and literary critics are united on this point and that each group of scholars shows respect for the methodology of the other means that they are engaged upon the common purpose of situating Spenser and his writings in their appropriate political, religious and social contexts so that his life and works can be more accurately interpreted. The principal value of this collection of essays is that it bears witness both to this new-found sense of common purpose and to the fruits that can derive from a united approach.

To say this is not of course to disregard the fact that historians and literary critics each cling to their own methodologies, and one of the fascinations of this collection is the extent to which the different approaches to a common scholarly subject are revealed. The most striking difference is that literary scholars devote almost exclusive attention to the text itself and seek to ascertain the author's meaning from the drift of argument and, when that fails them, from the form of the texts. Historians also devote attention to the text but they always reach beyond it for other evidence which will assist them in determining the purpose of the author. Thus in the present collection, we find Patricia Coughlan looking first to Spenser's prose and poetry and then to the dialogue form of his principal prose text to illustrate "the characteristic tensions in Spenser's thought".[3] Similarly with Anne Fogarty who reveals through a close scrutiny of the same text how Spenser employed language to impose an ordered appearance upon his discourse as also upon the society that he proposed to reform. In both instances the authors do move beyond the writings of Spenser to make reference to external evidence that will uphold their arguments but such reference is almost invariably to textual material rather than to historical events. Richard McCabe appears more ready than his two literary colleagues to move beyond the writings of Spenser but in doing so he too concentrates on texts. The first to which he makes reference is Machiavelli's *Prince* as he seeks to demonstrate how "necessity" when it was invoked by Machiavelli as a justification for action was fundamentally different from the "moral necessity" cited by Spenser to legitimize the measures that he considered appropriate for establishing an acceptable social order in Ireland. The second body of textual material, other than the writings of Spenser, to which Dr. McCabe makes reference are the compositions by Arthur, Lord Grey, and by the father of Lord Grey. These are cited by McCabe to establish a pedigree for the moral imperative that guided and motivated Edmund Spenser in his writings and actions.[4]

Whenever historians study the primary texts it is usually to isolate what they consider unique in Spenser's writing, or to alert their readers to what remained unsaid by him. Therefore in this volume Ciarán Brady is concerned to advance a plausible explanation as to why Spenser composed *A View of the Present State of Ireland* and why, when written, that work failed to obtain official approval for publication. Since these were matters on which Spenser himself remained entirely silent Brady seeks to provide answers by comparing the Spenser text with similar works by near contemporaries. Then having identified the elements that he considers to be the exclusive property of the Spenser text (and therefore those elements that are likely to have been found objectionable by the authorities), he proceeds to explain why Spenser took the position that he did by referring to the immediate political context in which Spenser executed his work. By this process Brady concludes that Spenser's dismissal of English common law as a possible instrument of reform would have caused offence to those in power in England. This alone, according to Dr. Brady, would explain why the *View* was denied publication during the reign of Queen Elizabeth.[5]

Most historians would accept this as plausible and would argue that this and other extreme recommendations were advanced by Spenser because he perceived himself and his fellow English-born officials in Ireland to be isolated both in relation to those who had real political influence in Ireland and those who controlled patronage in England. It is argued that this isolation, and the sense of powerlessness that derived form it, provoked Spenser to formulate radical proposals which would if implemented have placed himself, and the other English colonists in Ireland, in an undisputed position of authority.[6]

This explanation of the extreme character of Spenser's recommendations for Ireland appears plausible. The more significant for our present purpose however is the fact that the literary scholars whose work appears in this volume do not see the need to identify any particular aspects to Spenser's argument that would have rendered his entire text objectionable to Queen Elizabeth and her advisers. For the literary scholars the offensive nature of the text is apparent from its very language and especially from the language employed by Spenser in that infamous passage where he describes the starvation of the population in Munster that followed upon the military actions of Lord Grey.[7] Historians, who are more familiar with such gory descriptions in the every-day correspondence of the time, recognize that the use of such language in itself would not have condemned Spenser's *View* to oblivion.

On the other hand historians, while impressed with the polished prose in particular passages of Spenser's *View*, come away from it with the impression that it is an incomplete and hastily fashioned text. This is suggested to them by the fact that the discussion appears to have been well underway when the reader is introduced to it, and also because the two parties to the debate digress regularly from their main thread of argument. We learn from the literary scholars, however, that such seeming crudities are clever ploys designed either to retain the attention of the reader or to mask the revolutionary character of the proposals being advanced. It emerges also from the discussion conducted by the literary scholars on the form of the text that Spenser's *View of the Present State of Ireland* is a cleverly crafted work; a point that is established by them when they compare it with compositions of a similar character.[8]

When this conclusion of the literary scholars is linked with that of the historians Spenser's *View* emerges as a coherent text, devised to advance a particular argument which, in turn, was intended to serve a special purpose. The immediate target was the advancement of the English settler community in Ireland to the point where they would control that country's destiny. This advancement was, however, intended to promote an even greater end which was the transformation of Ireland into a truly Protestant society. Such a grand ambition was no more than was to be expected from one who has been described by a recent critic as an essentially "Protestant poet", and the desperate means which he prescribed for the attainment of that glorious end were consistent with the draconian measures which Spenser depicted in *The Faerie Queene* as essential to the attainment of moral perfection.[9]

The fulfilment of this ambition in the actual case of Ireland, as in the imagined world of *Faerie*, would have necessitated the destruction of property, society and persons. Spenser's religious fervour was so intense, however, that he suffered no qualms of conscience when he detailed a scheme which, in the words of Richard McCabe, would have effected the realization of "a Cromwellian dream a century before Cromwell".[10] In practical terms this would have involved the dispossession of all Catholic proprietors in Ireland, whether of Old English or Gaelic ancestry, the dissolution of the existing kinship groups in Ireland, and the resettlement of the indigenous population among a greatly augmented English planter community where they would together live under the tutelage of benevolent English lords. This new environment was considered conducive to bringing the native population to an acceptance of the Protestant faith, to an understanding of the English language, and to an involvement with a more individualist economy. Then, when this new order was established, it was to be held in place through the administration of the English common law which was considered appropriate for conserving an established civil order although not for creating one.[11] All of this appeared measured and humane, and seemed to be in complete accord with every known humanist programme of reform. Where it departed from such programmes was not in admitting that the desired reform was certain to encounter resistance but in detailing the gruesome military action that would be necessary to overcome such recalcitrance.

Literary scholars of previous generations had difficulty in reconciling these extreme measures, which were recommended by Spenser for the reform of Ireland, with his reputation as a gentle poet.[12] The present generation of literary scholars, as is apparent from the essays in this collection, experience no such difficulty and they accept that Spenser, like many others of his generation, could reveal an enthusiasm both for the humanist inheritance and for militant Protestantism. They can also accept that the supporter of either intellectual movement had of necessity to be an advocate of change because, as one author has put it, change had come "to be understood as the necessary condition of the process by which creatures move towards their perfection".[13] Students of literature are thus satisfied that when Spenser became an advocate of radical, and even revolutionary change he was remaining true to both intellectual traditions with which he identified.

Historians seem to experience greater difficulty in accepting that the two intellectual traditions could be reconciled. Indeed the particular concern of Dr. Brendan Bradshaw, in his recent writings on Spenser, has been to demonstrate that when Spenser became attached to the Calvinist doctrine of predestination he was rejecting the humanist inheritance to which he professed allegiance. The first of Bradshaw's publications which relates directly to this subject sets out to prove that Spenser's concept of justice, as exemplified in Book V of the *Faerie Queene*, was strongly influenced by Protestant theology and that the poem is "not only an allegory of human justice but an allegory of supernatural justification as well". The justification which Dr. Bradshaw has in mind is the Protestant doctrine of justification by faith alone and he contends that justice as depicted in the poem conforms

to the account of the three stages of justification discerned in the Protestant doctrine of salvation: predestination – election at the

church of Isis; conversion – at Radigund's castle; sanctification – at
the court of Mercilla.[14]

Some might argue that Dr. Bradshaw is reading more explicit dogma
into the poem than was intended by its author but nobody would dispute
his more general proposition that the *Faerie Queene* is an essentially Protestant poem "written with the issue of social order and social reform in
England at the centre of Spenser's pre-occupations". Neither would
anybody dispute Dr. Bradshaw's further contention that this same zeal
for the advancement of Protestant reform inspired Spenser to compose
A View of the Present State of Ireland, and most historians as well as
literary scholars would accept that this, like all reform texts of the sixteenth century, had ultimately to be justified on religious grounds.[15]
Where differences do emerge, however, is when Bradshaw further suggests that Spenser's *View* is the uniquely Calvinist text among all the
reform tracts relating to Ireland composed towards the close of the sixteenth century. Objection would also be raised to Bradshaw's more
explicit contention, developed in a separate article, that a necessary tension existed between humanist and Protestant reform and that one can
almost trace a decline of humanist idealism and its replacement by "stern
unbending Calvinism" as one studies the succession of reform texts that
appeared over the course of the sixteenth century. As Bradshaw depicts
it, the progress of Protestant zeal among the settlers in Elizabethan
Ireland had its culmination in Spenser's *View*. This he considers so far
removed from a reform text, in the Erasmian sense of that term, that he
describes it as a mere "rationale" for Spenser's "final solution" which
Bradshaw delineates in specific detail "to ensure that Spenser incurs . . .
the obloquy he deserves".[16]
Those who conceive the task of historians to consist in explaining,
rather than judging, events in the past may find rather disturbing this
exhortation to condemn the recommendations made by Edmund Spenser
for Ireland in 1596. Equally alarming to such people will be the use made
by Bradshaw and also by Ciarán Brady of such value-laden terms as the
"holocaust" and the "final solution" to describe what Spenser had in
mind for the Irish population, as also Bradshaw's description of the
Elizabethan state in Ireland as "totalitarian".[17] More specifically, in the
writings of Brendan Bradshaw, we are being led to believe that the adoption by policy makers of Calvinist theological belief, and their application of these beliefs to social and political affairs, led inevitably to

profoundly shocking conclusions. Clearly what is being suggested is that Spenser had so far departed from the ambitions of humanist reformers that he had come to the point where, like Hitler, he would embark upon genocide and that, in *A View of the Present State of Ireland*, he had outlined a programme similar to that delineated in *Mein Kampf*.[18]

This argument is in my opinion severely flawed first because it is based upon a misreading of Spenser's intentions and second because it assumes a moderation and a tolerance of diversity on the part of Erasmian humanist reformers that never existed. The emphasis which Erasmian humanists placed upon right learning, the scorn they poured upon all who did not comply with their own educational standards and the intolerance which they displayed towards those who challenged their opinions all cast doubt on their supposed moderation.[19] Erasmian humanists were, it is true, sharply critical of European attachment to warlike manners and to their pursuit of internecine war but they had no objection to European Christians mobilising their forces against Turk or heathen.[20] This, in itself, proves that humanists were not pacifists and they could even, like Spenser and his contemporaries, legitimise war on the grounds of utility and in the interest of adancing civil society at the expense of a more backward one. The most explicit enunciation of such a rationale comes from Sir Thomas More, who, we can assume, would be accepted by Dr. Bradshaw as a good example of Erasmian humanism.

More formulated his position on this subject when he described how the Utopians provided for a natural increase in their population. Then he stated, it was the practise of the Utopians that they

> enroll citizens out of every city and, on the mainland nearest them, wherever the natives have much unoccupied and uncultivated land, they found a colony under their own laws. They join with themselves the natives if they are willing to dwell with them. When such a union takes place, the two parties gradually and easily merge and together absorb the same way of life and the same customs, much to the great advantage of both peoples. By their procedures they make the land sufficient for both, which previously seemed poor and barren to the natives. The inhabitants who refuse to live according to their laws, they drive from the territory which they carve out for themselves. If they resist, they wage war against them. They consider it a most just cause for war when a people does not use its soil but keeps it idle and waste nevertheless forbids the use and posses-

sion of it to others who by the rule of nature ought to be maintained by it.[21]

This detailed explication by Thomas More reveals that he considered it eminently reasonable that civilized human beings should have resort to war with a view to asserting their authority over less-developed peoples whenever necessity dictated that this was the only course open to them. In this he was little different from Edmund Spenser and he was certainly not different from the succession of politicians, Old English and New English alike, who directed the course of events in Ireland from the 1530s forward to the mid-1850s. Those, or the majority of them, who have been portrayed by Dr. Bradshaw as Erasmian humanists, held the Gaelic society which they encountered in Ireland in utter disdain and they were willing to countenance any measures, short of total war, to effect its overthrow. This overthrow was with the purpose of absorbing the native population into an anglicized society where they would enjoy the benefits of an advanced economy, an enlightened legal system and a truly Christian religion.[22]

The fact that this succession of strategists recoiled from total war is explained by tactical reasons rather than by any principled objection to warfare. English-born officials were generally satisfied with half-measures because they accepted that the government of Queen Elizabeth would never provide the resources necessary for completing the reconquest of Ireland. At the same time the leaders of the Old English community, including those who held official positions under the crown, remained stridently opposed to a policy of reconquest because they recognized that any increase in militarization would result in themselves being displaced by Englishmen. Thus the two groups could unite on a scheme which aimed at the absorption of the Gaelic population in the country into an English-style order through the extension of the benefits of English law to all people within the country.[23]

Brendan Bradshaw has detailed, in his impressive work on the *Irish Constitutional Revolution of the Sixteenth Century*, how a consensus was arrived at between the Old and New English elements in the Irish government at the outset of the 1540s and how their programme of reform was proceeded with during the course of that decade.[24] That same author has also argued persuasively that this scheme was in accord with preferred humanist strategy although he has nowhere demonstrated that any of the supporters of this policy were directly associated with the humanist movement or were even conversant with humanist literature. Nonetheless, as is clear from the foregoing passage from More's *Utopia*, there is no need to quibble with Bradshaw's claims for a humanist ancestry for the new strategy for reform that was embraced by the Irish government in 1541, nor is this claim invalidated by the evidence, cited by Ciarán Brady in his present paper, that the advocates of this policy always envisaged that its application would involve a considerable degree of coercion.[25]

Time and experience were to reveal, however, that the task undertaken was more intractable, and more costly in terms of life and money, than had been envisaged by the enthusiasts of the 1540s. The issue became more complex·also when most English settlers in Ireland, like their kinsfolk at home in England, became attached to advanced Protestant opinion at the very time when the Catholic Old English in Ireland were being drawn closer to the doctrines as redefined at the Council of Trent. In these circumstances, the leaders of the Protestant official group refused to accept the Old English as allies in the pursuit of a common purpose, and some went to the extreme of stating that it was the religiously obdurate Old English rather than the primitive Gaelic Irish who were the principal obstacle to the achievement of a truly reformed society in Ireland. The obvious retaliation to this charge was that it was the English settlers themselves, because of their attachment to military measures, who had abandoned the path of reform.[26]

Thus in this atmosphere of charge and counter-charge was born the idea, which is now given fresh life by Drs. Brady and Bradshaw, that the great reform ambitions for Ireland that had first been formulated in the 1540s were abandoned at some point in the 1580s. To some extent this charge is true because the English government then did decide that it wished to cut its losses in Ireland and to concentrate instead on its domestic and continental involvements. For Ireland, this involved the abandonment of any ambition either to absorb the Gaelic community into an English-type society or to disarm the Old English provincial lords. This proposed curtailment of government activity met with the unqualified support of the leaders of the Old English community which meant that they also were withdrawing from their commitment to extend the benefits of English law to all elements of the population of Ireland.[27]

In this climate of disenchantment and loss of nerve it was the Protestant English-born officials and planters in Ireland who reminded the authorities in England of their special responsibility towards their second

kingdom. To ignore these responsibilities and to permit the Irish to continue in their ungodly state was, it was alleged, certain to provoke God
to bring severe punishment upon England itself and to place England's
tenuous control over Ireland in jeopardy.[28] These therefore became the
most persistent advocates of reform in Ireland, and if we take Spenser's
View of the Present State of Ireland as an example of this literature of
exhortation we find that it is truly ameliorative in intent because Spenser
commences his discourse with an onslaught against those who, having
despaired of reforming Ireland, would abandon the country to its own
devices. Such people were likened by Spenser to a physician who would
"wish his diseased patient dead rather than to apply the best endeavours
to his skill for his recovery". Then, continuing the medical analogy,
Spenser likened his own method to that of wise physicians who

> do first require that the malady be known thoroughly and dis-
> covered, afterwards to teach how to cure and redress it, and lastly
> to prescribe a diet with strait rules and orders to be observed for fear
> of relapse into the former disease or falling into some other more
> dangerous than it.

This opening reveals that Spenser intended to reform rather than to
destroy the people of Ireland and the suggestion that he departed sharply
from the reform tradition of the 1540s just does not accord with the
evidence. While being generally within this reform tradition, Spenser's
View (as also those other tracts which were composed by English settlers
in Ireland during the 1580s) charted a different course from those earlier
tracts for the attainment of a reformed society. The most apparent shift
from the traditional approach was in the insistence upon the primacy of
coercion in attaining a civil order. This, as we have seen, did not represent a total break with the previous consensus approach which had
always allowed for the employment of some force to attain the desired
objective. Now, however, force was identified as the essential instrument
of reform and it was stated explicitly that the educational and evangeliza-
tion aspects of the reform effort would necessarily be deferred until the
people had been cowed into submission and reorganized into an acceptable social order.[29]

While this new prescription for reform represented an undoubted
hardening of attitude over what had previously been current we do not
have to resort to some dubious socio-theological argument to explain this

change. Even the general reform scheme devised by Thomas More made allowance for the unqualified use of force when those who were to be embraced into a higher order proved themselves persistently hostile to change. If this model of Thomas More was in the minds of the reformers of the 1580s (and we have no proof that it was) they had plenty of evidence of obstinacy on the part of the Irish population to justify their change of emphasis within the reform strategy.[30]

Another reason behind this hardening of attitude was the fact that the task being undertaken by the reformers of the 1580s was altogether more formidable than that which confronted their predecessors of the 1540s. Those Englishmen who had belonged to the earlier reform movement enjoyed the support and encouragement of an influential element of the Old English population of the country, and they believed themselves to be engaged upon the purpose of extending the civil conditions of the Pale into the wider society beyond. Experience had convinced the English officials and settlers of the 1580s that no Englishman could place trust in Old English support. As a consequence the New English as a group concluded that only they were committed to the reform of Ireland, and that they would be forced to rely principally upon their own resources to achieve their reform ambitions.[31]

The task of the New English was also rendered more difficult by their conviction, already alluded to, that the Old English society in Ireland, no less than that of the Gaelic Irish, was in need of fundamental reform. This conclusion was inescapable for any committed Protestant who took account of the fact that the Old English population of the Pale and in the towns had become fully evangelized Catholics and were therefore less likely than the Gaelic Irish, who were recognized to be poorly instructed in any faith, to be brought to an acceptance of Protestant doctrine.[32] As a consequence, since the ultimate end to any reform drive was the attainment of a Protestant society, some New English were forced to recommend that their work should begin with an assault against all institutions which were under Old English control. Otherwise, it was argued, these institutions would be used to obstruct the reform effort among the Gaelic Irish as well as among the Old English population.[33]

This explanation of the factors that motivated Edmund Spenser to compose a text that related specifically to the reform of Ireland reveals that the intensification of religious zeal, on both sides of the sectarian divide, did influence attitudes towards reform, although not in the way that Dr. Bradshaw has suggested. There was, if anything, a renewal rather than a reduction in reform fervour, but this fervour was now focussed more explicitly on the ultimate religious end. As a consequence, the Old English were exposed to criticism in a way they had never been before, and the novelty of Spenser's *View* is not, as Bradshaw has suggested, the invective which it directed against Gaelic institutions but rather the vicious attack which it launched against the leaders of the Old English community and the policies which they had previously advocated.[34] Nor, it must be emphasised, did the New English Protestants escape unscathed, and Spenser, like his contemporary Sir William Herbert, devoted much effort to detailing how their compatriots had been lured from Christian civility by the ungodly license which was so pervasive in Ireland.[35]

Consideration of this phenomenon added to the conviction of Spenser and his contemporaries that societies which had fallen totally from the ways of civility could be reformed only through compulsion.[36] Furthermore, and this was one of the more important messages in Spenser's *View*, it was argued that any civil people who settled in such a society and who sought to achieve social amelioration through persuasive means would inevitably become absorbed into the corruption of their host community. This insistence upon the inevitability of decay might suggest that Spenser and his associates were being influenced by a Calvinist pessimism that evil would always prevail over good unless godly people remained constantly vigilant against it. This may indeed have been an influencing factor but, if so, it was never cited explicitly in the texts by the New English, where classical precedent and their own experiences in Ireland were always advanced as an explanation for their hardening of attitude as reformers.[37] The only departure from this was in those texts which were composed in the immediate aftermath of an Irish onslaught against the settler population, such as the "Supplication of the Blood of the English".[38]

Then, as was only to be expected from intensely religious people, the misfortune that had befallen the settlers in Ireland was attributed to God as a punishment both for their own evil living and for their neglect of God's purpose which was defined as the establishment of "the Gospel" in Ireland. To this extent the Irish, "that cursed seed of Esau" and "a perverse froward and stiffened generation", had become the "vessels of reprobation". Moreover, the author of the "Supplication of the Blood of the English" could see no hope that the settlers would be saved from further punishment unless they cast aside their ungodly ways and undertook the preaching of the Gospel by word and example. At the same time they were assured that when they directed themselves to godly purpose, they would be able to launch a second conquest and take their revenge upon those who had been directly responsible for the acts of brutality that had been directed against them. Those specifically identified as participants in this onslaught, and the Catholic clergy who had inspired them, were to be summarily put to the sword and these "loiterers being sifted out the labourers may be kept to manure the country". Any of these who had been directly involved in the depredations committed were to be made "slaves" to those "whose fellowship they could not abide under so gracious a prince in freedom", and it was further decreed that their children should "be always brought up to their fathers' labour". This terrible punishment was with the intention that "their life" would be a token of the queen's mercy "and their estate a remembrance of their own desert".

The tenor of this, and similar texts composed at the moment of overthrow, was highly charged with religious foreboding, but even in such fatalistic pronouncements the reform purpose was not entirely lost sight of. Thus it was also argued that the insurrection which had occurred had been permitted by God to provide "a fit opportunity to make a perfect reformed Common Wealth of that kingdom which was never like in the former estate to be reformed". In stating this it was assumed, as it had been by Spenser, that true reform could only come through conquest, and the responsibility of the conqueror was to "establish his conquest, religion, the law and the language of his own country without the which he can never have any firm footing". Those in Ireland who were to be given the opportunity of becoming members of this reformed Common Wealth were those who had "not yet grown to that stubborness that they will rather break than bend". Continuing with this metaphor of the forge the author of the "Supplication" decreed that all such neophytes should "feel the fire", but he then quickly explained that he meant

> not the faggot, as our poor brethren did in the reign of their idolatry but let them feel the force of such compulsion that either they may be forced to come to the true God for a refuge, or else for their rebellious hearts to perish with their idol.

Such conciliatory remarks reveal that reform sentiment was not entirely lost even in the revenge literature that was composed at the moment of rebellion. Even less so was it lost in the literature written when the settlers and their spokesmen were confident that they could, with assistance from England, direct the course of events in Ireland. Spenser's *View* was composed at such a juncture, and the purpose of this paper has been to highlight the optimistic aspect of the text, and to counter those who would represent it as a fundamentally negative settlement which had abandoned hope of bringing the population of Ireland to a reformed condition. In the course of pursuing these dual ambitions it has been insisted that Spenser's *View* cannot be excluded from the genre of reform literature simply because of his insistence on compulsion as the necessary instrument of reform. This is not to deny that Spenser recommended measures that were both extreme and intolerant, but so also did most other reformers in sixteenth-century Europe, both those who were Catholic and those who were Protestant and those who preceded and those who succeeded Spenser. Neither should this surprise us because social reformers are by definition engaged upon the business of categorization which involves them in declaring one social form to be superior to another. Such statements of preference could often be aided by the development of dramatic contrasts and these were invariably heightened when religious ambitions were linked with social ones. This truth, which seems apparent to literary scholars, would seem to be less clear to historians and perhaps it is likely to continue so until historians begin to follow the example of the literary scholars in giving more emphasis to the analysis of what Spenser actually said in his writings, and less to the reading they would wish to impose upon his utterances.

1. Pauline Henley, *Spenser in Ireland* (Cork, 1928).
2. Nicholas Canny, "Edmund Spenser and the Development of an Anglo-Irish Identity", *Yearbook of English Studies* 13 (1983), 1-19; Ciarán Brady, "Spenser's Irish Crisis: Humanism and Experience in the 1590s", *Past & Present* 111 (May 1986), 17-49; Brendan Bradshaw, "Edmund Spenser on Justice and Mercy" in *The Writer as Witness*, ed. Tom Dunne (Cork, 1987); Brendan Bradshaw, "Robe and Sword in the Conquest of Ireland" in *Law and Government under the Tudors*, ed. Claire Cross, D. M. Loades and J. J. Scarisbrick (Cambridge, 1988); Nicholas Canny and Ciarán Brady, "Debate: Spenser's Irish Crisis: Humanism and Experience in the 1590s", *Past & Present* 120 (August 1988), 201-15.
3. Patricia Coughlan, "Some Secret Scourge", p. 68.
4. Anne Fogarty, "The Colonization of Language"; Richard A. McCabe, "The Fate of Irena", and sources cited by McCabe in his notes 12 and 13.
5. Ciarán Brady, "The Road to the View", p. 42.
6. Canny, Spenser and the Development of an Anglo-Irish Identity", pp. 11-17.

7. See *View*, p. 104. The passage is discussed in detail in Anne Fogarty, "The Colonization of Language", p. 90.
8. See especially Patricia Coughlan, "Some Secret Scourge", pp. 59-67.
9. Anthea Hume, *Edmund Spenser: Protestant Poet* (Cambridge, 1984).
10. McCabe, "The Fate of Irena", p. 119; and for the reform dimension to the Cromwellian confiscation of Ireland see T. C. Barnard, *Cromwellian Ireland: English Government and Reform in Ireland, 1649-1660* (Oxford, 1975).
11. Canny, "Spenser and the Development of an Anglo-Irish Identity", pp. 4-7.
12. For example, see C. S. Lewis, *The Allegory of Love* (Oxford, 1936).
13. Hume, p. 184; for quite a different reconciliation between the poet and the political man see Stephen Greenblatt, *Renaissance Self-Fashioning: From More to Shakespeare* (Chicago, 1980).
14. Bradshaw (1987), p. 84; this point has been advanced in more general terms in Brendan Bradshaw, "Sword, Word and Strategy in the Reformation in Ireland", *The Historical Journal* (1978), 475-502.
15. Bradshaw (1987), pp. 85-7.
16. Bradshaw (1988), especially pp. 143, 154, 156, 158.
17. Bradshaw (1988), pp. 143, 156; Brendan Bradshaw, "The Beginnings of Modern Ireland" in *The Irish Parliamentary Tradition*, ed. Brian Farrell (Dublin, 1973), p. 83, and Brady, p. 32.
18. Bradshaw (1987 and 1988).
19. The most convenient anthology from the works of Erasmus is *The Essential Erasmus*, ed. and trans. John P. Dolan (New York, 1964).
20. Erasmus, "The Complaint of Peace" in *The Essential Erasmus*, ed. Dolan, pp. 177-204, esp. 201.
21. *The Yale Edition of the Complete Works of Saint Thomas More*, Vol. 4, *Utopia*, ed. Edward Surtz and J. H. Hexter, p. 137, with Latin text on facing page.
22. For examples see D. B. Quinn, ed. "Edmund Walshe's 'Conjectures' Concerning the State of Ireland [1552]" in *Irish Historical Studies* 5 (1947), 303-322; Nicholas Canny, ed., "Rowland White's 'Discourse touching Ireland', c.1569" in *Irish Historical Studies* 20 (1977), 439-463; Nicholas Canny, "Rowland White's 'The Dysorders of the Irishery' (1571)" in *Studia Hibernica* 19 (1979) 147-160.
23. This subject is treated succinctly in Ciarán Brady, "The Road to the *View*"; see also Steven G. Ellis, *Tudor Ireland: Crown, Community and the Conflict of Cultures, 1470-1603* (London, 1985), especially pp. 108-150, 228-277.
24. Brendan Bradshaw, *The Irish Constitutional Revolution of the Sixteenth Century* (Cambridge, 1979), especially pp. 189-257.
25. Brady, "The Road to the *View*", pp. 36-7.
26. Nicholas Canny, "Identity Formation in Ireland: the Emergence of the Anglo-Irish" in *Colonial Identity in the Atlantic World*, ed. Nicholas Canny and Anthony Pagden (Princeton, 1987), pp. 159-212, especially 164-176.
27. Nicholas Canny, *From Reformation to Restoration: Ireland, 1534-1660* (Dublin, 1987), 94-7.
28. Trollope to Walsingham, 12 Sept. 1585 (P.R.O., S.P. 63, vol. 85, no. 39); Trollope to Burghley, 26 Oct. 1587 (P.R.O., S.P. 63, vol. 131, no. 64).
29. Canny, "Spenser and the Development of an Anglo-Irish Identity", pp. 4-7.
30. Canny, *From Reformation to Restoration*, pp. 70-107.

31. Ellis, pp. 228-277.
32. This point is put explicitly in Spenser, *View*, especially pp. 84-7, 151-2, 161.
33. See *View*, p. 93.
34. Canny, "Spenser and the Development of an Anglo-Irish Identity".
35. William Herbert, *Croftus: sive de Hivernia liber*, ed. W. E. Buckley (Roxburghe Club, III, 1887), 38-40, 54.
36. See *View*, p. 93.
37. The most classical of the sixteenth-century reform texts was Richard Beacon, *Solon his Follie: Or, a politique Discourse Touching the Reformation of Commonweales Conquered, Declined or Corrupted* (Oxford, 1594), but Herbert *Croftus* and Spenser *View* also cite classical authors to lend authority to their argument.
38. Anonymous, "Supplication of the Blood of the English", ed. Willy Maley, in *Analecta Hibernica*, forthcoming. I am grateful to Mr Maley for supplying me with a typescript of this text, from which I quote in the next two paragraphs.
39. A particularly good example of Catholic social reform being promoted by means of compulsion is that in the Habsburg territories for which see R. J. N. Evans, *The Making of the Habsburg Monarchy 1550-1700* (Oxford, 1979), especially pp. 311-418.
40. The requirement that readers concentrate on what appears on the surface of Spenser's writings rather than delve for hidden meanings is insisted upon repeatedly in Paul J. Alpers, *The Poetry of The Faerie Queene*.

The Road to the View: On the Decline of Reform Thought in Tudor Ireland

CIARÁN BRADY

It is an irony, though hardly one which Spenser himself would have appreciated, that several of the proposals for which the *View of the Present State of Ireland* became notorious had long before been espoused by a group for whom he harboured an especial dislike: the Anglo-Irish feudal magnates. Spenser's idea of starving the rebel Irish into submission by means of a systematic scorched earth policy had been anticipated back in the 1530s by Robert Cowley, a spokesman for the Butlers of Ormond; so too had his plans to displace the native land-holders by extensive English plantations and his notion of constructing fortified garrisons throughout the country to defend the new settlements.[1] More importantly Spenser's justification for such extreme measures echoed that voiced by many among the Anglo-Irish nobility earlier in the century: for his assertion that all previous attempts to govern Ireland had failed and that a new conquest should be launched *ab initio* was the central contention of one of the most influential Anglo-Irish treatises of the 1530s, Patrick Finglas's "Breviate of the getting of Ireland and of the decay of the same".[2]

Such similarities between Spenser and his Anglo-Irish enemies are, of course, largely superficial: for it is evident that the magnates who presumed that they should take a leading role in the new conquest were the very group whom Spenser wished to exclude from all participation in the reconstruction of English rule in Ireland. Yet they are not entirely misleading, because the odd similarity of such views is the result of an equally polemical attitude which first the magnates, and later Spenser, assumed against what both perceived to be the official and wholly erroneous attitude of the English government in the resolution of its Irish problem. Both, that is, arose from the common conviction that the hope of making Ireland answerable to English rule by patient and gradual social reform was fundamentally wrong.

Wrong or not, however, the belief that Ireland could indeed be made governable, not by conquest but by means of legal and institutional reconstruction was, as Brendan Bradshaw has contended, based on sound and forcefully presented political argument. Such a policy, Bradshaw has argued, issued from a small group of politically active lawyers and administrators within the English Pale in Ireland who tirelessly plied Henry VIII and his councillors throughout the 1520s and 1530s with treaties and memoranda urging the abandonment of old claims to conquest and the adoption of a boldly original conciliatory initiative. Eventually, and due to the highly influential support of the king's close companion, Sir Anthony St. Leger, they convinced King Henry of their case; and the crown's commitment to attempt the revival of English rule in Ireland through the gradual education of the native ruling powers in the forms and procedures of the English common law was officially inaugurated in the legislative programme of the Irish parliament of 1541.[3]

Bradshaw's account of the travail and triumphs of the Pale's political reformers is immensely attractive but there are important senses in which his case has been overstated. The conciliatory and peaceful objectives of such writings were rarely unalloyed and frequently they conceded the necessity of force and dispossession in some areas, and its desirability in others. More importantly, however, emphasis upon the original and revolutionary character of the Palesmen's propositions may tend to obscure the extent to which their ideas were rooted in the deeply conservative tradition of English common-law thought. For at the core of their view that a conquest was unworkable and should be abandoned was the far more positive assumption that the law itself could accomplish what sheer might had failed to achieve.

Such a case was maintained on a number of levels. A new conquest, they argued, was for a variety of financial, logistical and diplomatic reasons so risky as to be quite impracticable. But it was unnecessary for the rather less obvious reason that the earlier effort at conquest had already achieved all that might be expected from such an approach. It had broken the power of the native Irish lords, destroyed whatever political and diplomatic structures had existed under the Gaelic high-kings and thereby confirmed the superiority of English law and its right to be established throughout the island.[4]

That such claims had been effectively established in practice was evident in the survival of English legal institutions in the Pale, the corporate towns and until most recently in large tracts of Munster and Connacht. This rapid contraction of English law in Ireland, however, was interpreted by these writers to be a sign not of the failure of the conquest, but rather as a demonstration of the essential limitations of such a simple strategy. For having once established their military and political dominance in the island, the descendants of the Anglo-Norman conquerors had exploited their superiority not to defend or extend English law, but simply to increase their own power and wealth. Thus when the requirements of law came into conflict with their own private interests they quickly abandoned it and embraced instead the lawless system of extortion, protection and intimidation which the reform writers labelled "coyne and livery".

The old colonists' relatively recent adoption of "coyne and livery" was, all of the reform writers were agreed, the fundamental cause of the decay of English rule in Ireland and it was on this central assumption that all their propositions rested. It was for this reason that they rejected outright the strategy of a new conquest: it would in all likelihood simply strengthen the position of certain Anglo-Irish lords upon whose support and cooperation the crown would inevitably be dependent. But even if properly supervised at first it would eventually fall victim to the same degeneration that had beset the old conquest. For this reason also they advocated the apparently contradictory policies of introducing new English settlements in strategic areas, and of cultivating the goodwill of certain powerful Gaelic Irish lords; for each of these measures provided a means of dissolving the influence of the great networks of clientage set up under the aegis of "coyne and livery". But it was for this reason above all that they urged the revival and extension throughout the country of the instruments of common law which, though now under threat, had been the chief maintainers of English political culture in Ireland for almost four hundred years.

Certain distinctions have been noted among these reform writers: distinctions between those who argued that a general plan be implemented over the whole island and those who confined themselves to a more limited set of objectives, between those who were confident that the majority of the native Irish could be won over peacefully to reform, and those who were not.[6] Yet it is unclear whether such differences of opinion were deeply rooted or whether they arose simply from the practical circumstances in which many of the reform tracts were written and the immediate objectives they were designed to meet. But these writings all showed the common conviction that the restoration of English rule in Ireland could be accomplished in full only through the thorough exploitation of those legal and administrative structures already established in Ireland and available for wider application. Such confidence in the efficacy of law did not, however, imply a rejection of the use of force. There had always been a distinctly coercive element in the operation of English common law, particularly on the criminal side; and several of the reform proponents were agreed that respect for due process was best inculcated in the most lawless parts of the land by the establishment of provincial councils which would enjoy wide jurisdictional and administrative powers acting under commissions of peace and of *oyer and terminer*.[7] But the advocacy of such instruments of regional government merely underlined the conventional legalistic character of the reformers' thought, for it was precisely by these means that King Henry's closest advisers had hoped to revive respect for the law within outlying areas of England itself.

It is arguable, therefore, that it was the conservative rather than the innovative character of Irish reform thought – its confidence in the essential efficacy of conventional institutions and procedures when properly applied rather than its demand for some boldly original strategy – that made it familiar and attractive to the Henrician government. But the consequences of its success in winning control of English policy for Ireland were no less profound for that. For from at least the early 1540s through to the middle of the 1580s successive English administrators operated under the assumption that they could gradually extend the Dublin government's control over the whole island through the employment of the same instruments and procedures which worked with such apparent efficiency in England itself. And they were made all the more confident in this assumption by the fact that its validity had been confirmed by the advocacy of the most experienced and most loyal English community in Ireland, the lawyers and administrators of the Pale.

This long-term project of institutional reconstruction was repeatedly disrupted by inadequate financing, internal administrative wrangles and unexpected resistance often of a most violent kind. Progress was slow, far slower than even the most cautious had anticipated, and frustration with the results of their efforts mounted palpably among administrators through the middle decades of the century. But for all that commitment to the essential elements of the reform programme remained strong. The offices of the central administration were resuscitated by alterations in personnel and procedure, assize circuits were revived and extended; commissions of peace were established in areas where they had never operated before; diplomatic arrangements with Gaelic chieftains concerning the adoption of primogeniture as a mode of inheritance for power and property were secured, new shires were gradually created and provincial councils, after several false starts, were at length introduced in Munster and Connacht in the early 1570s. Most importantly of all, perhaps, the summoning of successively more representative parliaments in Dublin for the passage of a long series of statutes concerned with the mechanics and particular details of reform provided the most overt indication that the achievement of political and social change by means of law remained a central aim of government.[8]

The reform policy's capture of the citadel of government could be noted in a somewhat less obvious manner in a change in the character of advice proffered to governors by political commentators within Ireland. Thus figures like Sir Thomas Cusack and Sir John Alen, both of whom had proffered often different but equally general analyses of the island's political problems in the past, tended in the latter part of their careers to restrict themselves to specific administrative or diplomatic recommendations. Similarly the Palesman who was the author of a lengthy set of memoranda for Lord Deputy Sussex in the late 1550s (possibly the Attorney-General James Barnewall) confined himself to the highly practical issue of making the governor's management of finances more efficient.[9] Even more suggestive is the case of Rowland White, that inveterate boaster whose proposals for social and political improvement multiplied in inverse relation to his own declining fortunes. Though his mind bristled with a great variety of reform ideas, White chose to present his proposals uniformly as a series of draft parliamentary bills for which he supplied extensive preambles. White's choice of form thus indicated that as late as the early 1570s, the Irish parliament was regarded, as it had been in the 1540s, as the principal means by which the crown's law was made amenable to the subject and the subject to the law.[10]

That White's view of the role of parliament was shared by the government itself could be seen from the official legislative programme placed by Sir Henry Sidney before a parliament which sat as White made his last proposals. From the beginning of his service in 1565 Sidney had hoped to summon a parliament for the purposes of reviewing the impetus of reform, and though he was forced to wait until 1569, the draft legislation he presented to the parliament then convened constituted a renewal of the government's commitment to legal reconstruction. New statutes proclaimed Sidney's intent to establish shire government throughout the country, to institute tenurial reform on a systematic basis, to introduce English customs of inheritance and to bring about the abolition of the bane of coyne and livery. The lengthy preamble to one of the earliest pieces of major legislation, the act for the attainder of Shane O'Neill, made clear the general context within which the other bills were to be seen. Having recounted the principal claims by which the English crown enjoyed title to Ireland, emphasising those arising both from the old conquest and from the Kingship Act of 1541, the preamble declared that the Irish people's heartfelt desire for order and justice, though long frustrated, was about to be satisfied by the new legislation Sidney had prepared for them.[10] The parliament's actual reception of some of Sidney's proposals, most notably his scheme to establish a university in the Pale, was rather more negative than he had expected. But even as he somewhat disappointedly addressed its final session, Sidney repeated his commitment to the conventional reform policy. The legislation passed was indeed beneficial to the crown, he agreed, but only in so far as it benefitted the Irish subjects themselves, for "whatsoever this benefit amounts to, it returns to yourselves in a circle, here it is grown, here it is eaten, here it multiplies, here it is spent".[11]

Fifteen years later Lord Deputy Sir John Perrot was to suffer the indignity of seeing an equally ambitious legislative programme bedevilled by sustained opposition, yet even at the close of this turbulent parliament the Speaker of the Commons, Sir Nicholas Walsh, could address the house in the language of conventional legal reform. Recalling the establishment of a united kingdom in Ireland in 1541 and praising the work of the parliament in sustaining the health of the Irish constitution, Walsh explicitly cited Sir John Fortesque's "De Laudibus Legem Anglie", the standard text of English constitutional thought, as the authority for his contention that the common law of England provided the best possible basis for any political system and for his hope that through the efforts of the governor and the cooperation of the subjects it might be extended to all Ireland.[12]

Walsh's peroration, however, was not entirely unqualified. His speech was peppered with ambiguous references to New English "impes" and to that highly charged phrase "the country cause".[13] He lamented also that the benefits of the queen's "bounty and grace do not yield so comfortable a heat here as they do nearer unto the Highnesses person", and prayed that Ireland should henceforth be no longer treated as "an instrument without a sounding board". These dissonances, however muted, were, given the context in which they were made, highly significant; for they heralded the emergence in parliament, the very centre-piece of the new Irish constitution, of a deep disquiet that had begun to be expressed by Irish-born reformers even as their central arguments had gained acceptance as the ruling orthodoxy.

This rising unease could be seen at work even in the writings of the irrepressible Rowland White.[14] As he plied the government with positive legislative proposals, White nevertheless expressed disappointment that the project launched with enthusiasm in the 1540s had so rapidly become the source of recrimination and dispute. The source of the rising antagonism between the government and its ostensibly loyal supporters, White argued, could be traced not to any fundamental flaw in the objectives of the reform policy upon which both sides were agreed, but rather to the methods by which the government set about achieving them, to the routine conduct that is of the Dublin administration, and of the army in particular. By the time he made them, however, White's criticisms had become commonplace among Pale political writers. They had been anticipated by the Marian primate of Armagh, George Dowdall, who launched a vigorous attack not on the aims of Sussex's government, but on his personal conduct as viceroy, and by William Bermingham, another Pale commentator whose positive suggestions for the improvement of the crown's Irish finances were based wholly upon a sharp critique of the extravagance, abuses and corruptions of Sussex's officer corps.[15] But perhaps the most interesting example of the rising disillusion is presented by the case of Edward Walshe.

The author in the mid-1540s of an enthusiastic pamphlet urging all Irishmen to contribute to, or participate in, Henry VIII's French wars, Walshe had grown markedly unhappy with the administration of King Henry's Irish kingdom by the early 1550s. In his "Conjectures on the state of Ireland'' (1552), Walshe was severely critical of the manner in which Dublin administrators had become susceptible to particular local influences which despite their protestations of loyalty, were not supportive of the crown's reform aims. Some through corruption, others through sheer obtuseness and others again through a misplaced pride were unwilling to admit their mistake; but they were all, for whatever reason, responsible for the deflection of the government's objectives. To remedy this Walshe advocated the establishment of several small, densely planted settlements which would be like the old Roman colonies economically and militarily self-sufficient. By the later 1550s, however, after Lord Deputy Sussex had established a new plantation scheme in Leix-Offaly based upon a set of militarily secure garrisons, Walshe's disillusion with the government had grown even deeper. This alternative approach was also unacceptable, because, Walshe argued, it had allowed a narrow military caste to exercise too much influence over the government, rendering it more insensitive to the needs of the loyal subjects and too tolerant of the corruption and abuses of the soldiers.[16]

Thereafter Walshe relapsed into silence and with the exception of White and (partially) Bermingham proposals for further reform ceased to issue from the Pale. Instead, articulations of political opinion in Ireland began to take on a pronounced oppositional tone, such as in the long series of charges made by the Pale law students against Sussex in 1561 or in the lampoons directed at Sidney during the time of his parliament, and most notably in the carefully-argued constitutionalist complaints of the ''common-wealth men'' of the 1570s. The sources of the several complaints have been explored elsewhere: they arose, it appears, in large part from the rising cost of billeting and supplying the army which the community of the Pale was being asked to bear, and from the government's manifest incapacity to prevent the extortions of the soldiers.[17] But what is relevant here is the mode in which these grievances were cast and the implications to which it gave rise. Arguing their case as loyal subjects of the kingdom of Ireland, obedient to its laws and institutions, they claimed equal entitlement to the same rights and freedoms as were enjoyed by the subjects of the sister-kingdom of England and they appealed directly to Queen Elizabeth as the sovereign of both realms to ensure that their liberties were preserved and their just complaints attended to.

Such an argument presented a grave challenge to the Dublin administration. In practical terms alone this direct appeal to the queen and the London government seriously weakened the credibility of the Irish viceroy at court and rendered him vulnerable to all manner of intrigues. More seriously it overtly denied the viceroy's claims to be fully representative of sovereignty in Ireland to whom alone all requests for favour and redress should be addressed and from whom alone communication would be made to the crown. But most serious of all, in their requests for royal intervention in Ireland the common-wealth men explicitly charged the Dublin governor with wilfully disregarding their status as free-born subjects which was the very basis on which their authority within the Irish kingdom rested.

It was this imputation that the Dublin governors were reneging upon their principal obligation to respect the rights of subjects under the reformed Irish constitution that made the conflict between the Palesmen and the governors particularly rancorous and personal from the outset. To the governors, those who complained against them were simply malcontents, political intriguers and eventually "arrant papists"; to the complainants the governors were profit-seeking adventurers and freebooters, men who had taken the land of Ireland out of contract. There was, on both sides, a great deal of exaggeration, misunderstanding and unwarranted suspicion. Yet ironically these bitterly maintained oppositions were founded upon the very wide ground of agreement on general principles which both sides shared. Because both sides believed in the regenerative capacity of English political culture in Ireland, because both were convinced that the carefully planned reconstruction of common-law institutions was the best way of ensuring orderly government in the island, and because both assumed that this should not be a markedly difficult or lengthy process, each could rationalise the appearance of unexpected but manifest difficulties in the reform project only in terms of a failure of commitment on the part of the other.

The inescapable corollary of Irish grievances against the army's misconduct, therefore, was an equally sharp claim from the governors that the English of Irish birth were themselves obstructive and disloyal, not suitable partners in the reform campaign to which they paid lip-service. In the 1560s such complaints generally took the shape of exasperated reports to the governors' superiors in London. But in the 1570s, as resistance to the army grew, they began to assume the form of systematic investigations into the familial, political and factional connections of Pale lawyers and administrators.

This growing conviction on the part of English administrators that their erstwhile partners in reform were now reneging upon their commitments, sacrificing the long-term interest of the English community in Ireland for the protection or advancement of their private concerns, considerably altered the way in which the administrators viewed the prospects of reform. For some, like Lord Chancellor Gerrard, the unsoundness of the Palesmen meant that any hope of extending English law throughout the country in the near future was futile. The corruption of English political culture had run far deeper than earlier commentators had allowed and had penetrated to the English of the Pale even as reform was supposedly getting under way. The national scheme now in operation was premature and should be suspended while the government concentrated its efforts on a thorough reform of the Pale itself. The management of the Dublin courts and of the assize circuits was to be placed in the hands of newly-arrived English lawyers. New English settlers and administrators were to be placed in prominence on local commissions of peace and native-born lawyers and officers were to be readmitted to places of influence only when they had given clear evidence that they were free from suspicion of political or familial partiality. The reform programme, therefore, needed to be radically retimetabled, and only when solid foundations had been established in the Pale could the proposed further advance be contemplated.[18]

Gerrard's contention that the Palesmen be excluded from the implementation of government policy was widely shared among fellow English administrators. But his highly restrictive view of the proper area of government operations was not: for few of his colleagues believed that a withdrawal of resources to the Pale was strategically practicable. Continuing disturbances among the great families in Munster and Connacht, the chronic guerrilla war in the midlands and the continuing threat of the O'Neill in Ulster demanded a highly active governmental presence in every province and any sign that the government was reducing its obligations outside the Pale to mere containment, as Gerrard had suggested, would simply provoke an even greater offensive against the small portion over which the crown still laid claim. Yet while they retained the conventional extensive view of the scope of reform, these administrators adopted a radically different attitude toward its mode of implementation. Because the establishment of English rule in Ireland was now more urgent than ever, but because neither the Gaelic Irish nor the Anglo-Irish could be counted upon to further its establishment by cooperation and accommodation, reform would have to be imposed on Ireland by force alone. Thus an increasing number of provincial governors and administrators argued that it was both necessary and legitimate for them to enforce their authority, and the authority of the law, by coercive means when persuasion failed.[19]

The emergence of this new tough attitude on the part of regional administrators has been related by a number of modern historians to the influence of ideas derived from the Spanish colonisation of the Americas.[20] The identification of the Gaelic Irish and degenerate Anglo-Irish with the primitive Amerindians who could be tutored into civilization only through extreme coercion, it has been argued, allowed the English to operate without the normal legal restraints, suppressing dissent and securing obedience by terror alone. Yet overt comparisons with the new world experience were, as one of their most careful analysts has conceded, scattered, and lacking in coherent argument.[21] In view of the obvious ideological advantages attached to such identifications, their relative scarcity is odd; and yet there were a number of important factors inhibiting the development of this line of argument.

To begin with, it was not easy to sustain practical comparisons between the Irishman and the Indian. For the English and Irish did not meet across a frontier but mingled closely together in a manner which overcame or diluted such cultural differences as existed between them. More importantly, the principal challenges to English rule, it was now clear, issued not from the Gaelic Irish, but from the Anglo-Irish and their relations in the Pale who could not easily be shown to stand comparison with native Americans. But the idea that England's rule in Ireland could be perceived as similar to that of Spain in America remained underdeveloped primarily because few of those involved in the administration of Ireland were as yet willing to pursue the implications which such a comparison raised. To have pointed to Ireland as England's colonial frontier would have been to deny all the assumptions inherent in the statutory recognition of Ireland's status as a kingdom in 1541. It would have denied, consequently, the validity of the Tudors' persistent efforts to govern Ireland by means of law, denied also the capacity of England's legal institutions to work reform in Ireland, and denied most importantly the very ability of the English common law to survive in a country in which it had long since been planted.

These radical implications, inevitably, induced caution among experienced English administrators when they moved to present their opinion in a formal manner. Thus despite his boastful account of his ruthless conduct while on campaign in Munster, Humphrey Gilbert's recommendations for the reform of the province were relatively moderate. Though deeply distrustful of the native population in general and anxious to have strong garrisons established throughout the region, Gilbert nonetheless proposed that the goodwill of the towns be cultivated, and suggested that the nobility could be made comfortable to law by long residences at the royal court, which were to be encouraged through generous exchanges of crown lands in England.[22] Similarly Sir John Perrot who was likewise convinced that political order could be enforced only by firm government, recommended that the regional governor should carefully cultivate the confidence and goodwill of the people by impartiality and by a sincere concern with the provision of justice.[23]

The classic presentation of this new approach to the reform of Ireland was made by Sidney's secretary Edmund Tremayne in a series of memoranda written in the early 1570s. Starting from the premise that the Anglo-Irish and the Palesmen were corrupt and could not be counted on, despite their protestations, to further the course of reform, Tremayne nonetheless contended that reform could be implemented by the employment of a group of short-term servitors, soldiers, administrators, lawyers and clerics who would act under the direction of the governor and who would be regularly replaced before they could acquire connections in the country. The central instrument of Tremayne's reform scheme was to be the army. The army, distributed in large numbers throughout the provinces was to enforce English forms of land tenure and inheritance under threat of extortion and even when the conventional institutions and procedures of common law had been accepted, the army would remain, albeit with greatly reduced strength, to ensure continuing respect for the English legal system.[24]

In its uncompromising defence of intimidation, Tremayne's argument appeared to be boldly innovative, and yet at heart it remained consistent with traditional reform thought. Tremayne, like Perrot, rejected another attempt at full conquest as impracticable and unnecessary, and surprisingly perhaps, he discounted the use of colonial settlements, which he believed would produce only another self-interested political faction. Tremayne's critique, therefore, was focussed not upon the central objective of Tudor reform thought, but rather upon the techniques that had been applied to bring it to fruition. Despite the marked increase in tough talk, the unashamed advocacy of force as a means of establishing reform, and denunciations of the unwillingness of the Irish and the perfidy of the Anglo-Irish, confidence in the ultimate success of patient administrative reform remained high. Sidney, though he had become sharply intolerant of obstruction from the Anglo-Irish, made a final effort to introduce political and tenurial reform in the provinces in the late 1570s by the methods Tremayne had advocated; and in the mid-1580s Sir John Perrot repeated the experiment with immense energy and determination.

As Sidney's and Perrot's efforts successively ended in failure and as the crown's troubles multiplied through rebellion in Munster (1579-83) and through chronic disorders in Connacht and the Pale throughout the 1580s, a further declension in the character of reform thinking began to become apparent. At its least significant this withdrawal of confidence in the prospect of reform could be seen in the unrelievedly negative criticism of the publicist Barnaby Rich who relentlessly catalogued the corruptions and deficiencies of both the native communities and the English administrators.[25] Though they offered little in the way of positive alternative proposals, other than the need to suppress corruption and cultivate virtue, Rich's fusillades doubtless reflected and contributed to a deepening disillusion with the entire record of government reform. In the same way, the occasional reports of Andrew Trollope, a travelling preacher who denounced in highly critical terms the failure of the religious reformation in Ireland, further underlined the government's lack of achievement in promoting cultural change, though again Trollope's own writings were never sufficiently integrated to allow for the presentation of a fully developed analysis.[26]

Rather more substantial reorientations in political thinking could be discerned in the systematic treatises composed by the Munster planter Sir William Herbert, in the late 1580s, and the Munster civil administrator Richard Beacon, in 1594. Beacon and Herbert were both sharply critical not only of the natives but also of successive English administrators who had failed to impose order upon them through idleness or corruption. Both insisted upon the necessity of coercion, praised those officers who had employed it effectively in the past, and attempted to provide a theoretical defence for its continued application in the Irish provinces.

In the latter treatise *Croftus sive de Hibernia* Herbert advocated radical territorial reorganization: he wanted the native communities reconstructed into villages and shires with English officers appointed to impose the law and to maintain order at each level. Those Irish who resisted reform, Herbert argued, were to be compelled to accept it, or to suffer dislodgement and transplantation. Despite this, however, Herbert remained confident that no institutions other than those of the common law "by which England has been brought and elevated to the highest point of perfection and to extraordinary happiness would be more preferable or more suitable to Ireland" and that the native Irish would come after a proper period of firm tutelage to see the truth of this.[27]

Beacon's *Solon his Follie* was more radical and more comprehensive in its advocacy of violence. Drawing heavily though without acknowledgement on Machiavelli's *Discourses on Livy*, Beacon argued that attempts to reform political cultures that had become totally corrupt by means of law alone were doomed to failure. In such conditions where lawlessness had become rife, respect could be instilled not by reason and consensus but by fear alone, and the officers of government should be freed from the normal legal restraints in their efforts to infuse that respect. Though his treatise was ostensibly a theoretical discussion of the role of law in the government of different states, with Solon the lawgiver acknowledging that law could not work the same effects in the corrupt polity of Salamina (the small island neighbour of the Athenian republic) as it did in Athens itself, Beacon interrupted his allegory to provide an explicit defence of Sir Richard Bingham as governor in Connacht. Though Bingham had recently been subject to severe criticism for his ruthless conduct in the province, Beacon argued that the governor had succeeded where all his predecessors had failed because he had recognised the truly degenerate state of his province and had adapted his strategy to accord with its norms. Only when Bingham's methods were officially acknowledged and extended elsewhere in Ireland would the country be made amenable to the rule of law.[28]

Beacon's case for the long-term application of repression represented a significant attack on the common assumption of Tudor policy in Ireland. And his argument was all the more effective in that it seemed to be based not on personal, and therefore questionable, experience as were so many recent criticisms, but on the sound foundations of political theory. Yet despite its pretensions to an abstract validity, his argument remained ambiguous at certain key points. Though he claimed that the government of Ireland was confronted by an absolutely degenerate political culture, it was not clear whether he regarded this degeneration as comprehensive or irreversible. He accepted, for instance, that the Gaelic Irish had been amenable to legal reform no more than twenty-five years ago and that the opportunity had been missed only through the negligence and incompetence of successive governors. Ireland's corruption, then, was not intrinsic, but something which had only recently developed through neglect, and which could now be recovered by sustained attention. Similarly despite his general condemnation of the native élites Beacon conceded that certain great lords remained sympathetic to reform, and warned that this select group should not be further alienated by indiscriminate and inflexible coercion. The corruption, therefore, was not pervasive, and the application of the cure, by implication, should be carefully judged. Such qualifications somewhat weakened the theoretical potential of Beacon's argument. But they allowed him to concentrate his argument on the importance of executive efficiency, which had been so neglected in the past, without committing him to a fundamental rejection of the view that the common law could work reform in Ireland.[29]

Beacon's avoidance of an overt attack on conventional reform thought was designed to make his case for the application of coercion seem more plausible and more influential. But even by the time he published (1594) his plea for the use of extended coercive policing, it was rendered irrelevant by the radical and wholly unexpected reaction which Bingham's aggression had provoked in Ulster and north Connacht.

The spread of rebellion in the north and west between 1593 and 1596 gave rise to a renewal of arguments for a thorough and permanent resolution to England's problem in Ireland. Demands for a purely military solution abounded, but in their midst there emerged also a far more considered critique of the failure of all other reform strategies that had been applied to Ireland in the past. Such was Spenser's *View of the Present State of Ireland*. With Tremayne, Perrot and so many others, Spenser shared a deep mistrust of the English of Irish birth, regarding them as even more dangerous and less tractable than the Gaelic Irish. Like Beacon, Spenser vigorously defended the enforcement of order through ruthless suppression, exonerating Lord Grey de Wilton from charges of needless cruelty and representing him as a singular figure who truly had grasped the real nature of England's difficulty in Ireland.

But Spenser went much further than previous writers and placed these by now common complaints in the context of a far more fundamental attack on the reform policy than had yet been made. For Spenser the failure of English law in Ireland had been due not to the recalcitrance or duplicity of individual native lords, nor to the incompetence or corruption of individual English governors, but to a systematic process of perversion which began to infect the procedures and institutions of the common law as soon as they were introduced into Ireland. Thus, as Spenser was at pains to show, English legal procedures, such as trial by jury, process in relation to the trial of accessories to felony, and the toleration of enfeoffments to trust, which had proved so beneficial in England, had not only failed in Ireland, but had actually contributed to the deterioration of order there. In attempting to reform Ireland by making it answerable to English laws, the sixteenth-century governors had, by a terrible irony, only succeeded in furthering the country's degeneration.

The explanation which Spenser provided as to the origins of this fundamental paradox was satisfactory neither on empirical nor on normative grounds. His argument that the communities of Ireland had become addicted to the political and social mores of their most primitive elements, the descendants of the nomad Scythians, was unsupported by any account of how this addiction came about, but was also in open contradiction to his own assertion that the most dangerous threat to English rule in Ireland emanated not from the Gaelic Irish, but from the powerful Anglo-Irish lords and the ostensibly loyal subjects of the Pale.[30]

But for all its internal difficulties Spenser's argument launched a powerful case against the maintenance of the traditional reform policy and in favour of the adoption of a wholly radical approach. The failure of English law in sixteenth-century Ireland could thus be explained not in terms of individual betrayals and surrenders, but confronted directly as the result of the fundamental inappropriateness of the common law to an exotic political culture. Once this had been established all further investment in the old policy of introducing English law to the Irish would be revealed as folly, and the need to set about the complete destruction of Ireland's existing political culture would replace it as the first priority of English government in Ireland. Only when that had been achieved and the Irish had been reduced, through mass starvation, exemplary killing and the imposition of full military repression, to a state of being without a culture at all could the process of educating them in the ways of the superior English culture commence.

The argument of the *View* was devised, therefore, as a means of making the abandonment of reform acceptable to those who had been its most consistent supporters, the confident upholders of the universal virtues of the English common law. The *View* is composed as a closely argued dialogue, in which Eudoxus, Spenser's second interlocutor, is no mere sounding-board for the ideas of the experienced Irish hand, Irenius, nor a naif, ignorant of the problems of government or of the recent English experience in Ireland. He is instead a representation of revised reform opinion, critical of past government failures, willing to apply severity when necessary, but forever optimistic concerning the curative powers of English political culture. In their debate, moreover, he is by no means subordinate to Irenius, remaining coolly unconvinced of his case until far into the argument and raising a number of objections which Irenius counters only after apparent difficulty. The dramatic pretence of the dialogue form was adopted by Spenser because it was imperative for him to show that when confronted with a true interpretation, a view, of the means by which Ireland came to its present condition, the sensitive, informed and critical English intelligence would concede the complete failure of its own central assumptions regarding the reform of Ireland, as in due course Eudoxus does.

With Spenser the strategic argument concerning the reimposition of English rule in Ireland appears to have turned full circle. Like the Anglo-Irish spokesmen of the earlier part of the century, Spenser implicitly conceded that the twelfth-century conquest had not completed its work, and that it was time to start anew, and like them also he urged that the subjugation of the native peoples be accomplished in the most ruthless and thorough manner. But unlike the Irish, Spenser was compelled to confront directly the central principle which had guided the course of English policy in Ireland since the 1540s: the contention that having once been planted the common law could only bring peace and prosperity to the territory over which it governed. Such a challenge was an enormous one, and it was to meet it that all the argumentative and rhetorical devices of the *View* were designed. For all that, as we know, Spenser failed, and after years of redrafting his text was refused publication by the Master Stationers in 1598, to remain unpublished for the next thirty-five years. But when seen in relation to his extraordinaryily ambitious intent Spenser's failure becomes more comprehensible. It has sometimes been contended that it was his unambiguous advocacy of naked force that provoked a response of embarrassed silence from those men of affairs whom he had hoped to influence, or more sceptically, that it was his honest declaration of the real bases of English power in Ireland that produced the same reaction.[31] Yet a simpler, though perhaps deeper, explanation would seem nearer the truth. Spenser's assault upon Irish reform was unacceptable not simply because it underlined the costly failure of successive English administrations in Ireland, but because it asserted that the great law itself lay at the source of this failure. The implications of such a charge were as intolerable to Lord Burghley or to Sir Edward Coke as they were to Elizabeth; but more seriously they proved to be equally so to the author himself.

Having justified his case for the abandonment of reform and the application of force on the grounds that "laws ought to be fashioned unto the manners and condition of the people to whom they are meant and ought not to be imposed upon them according to the simple rule of right" (*View*, p. 11), Spenser proceeded to argue that following the period of repression English laws and institutions would take root easily in the country. Thus the last part of the *View* rehearses the conventional reform proposals concerning land tenure, inheritance, religion, education and social organisation. Here at the close of his argument was a calming reassurance that, for all his radical criticisms, the author remained a stout believer in the virtues of the best constitution the world had ever known.

Yet Spenser was compelled to ask himself, through Eudoxus, just why total repression would make the people amenable to English law where conciliation and education had failed. His attempts to respond to this question involved Spenser in a hopeless tangle. He claimed first that since conditions in Ireland were now similar to those prevailing in England on the eve of the coming of the Normans, the system of government imposed by the Normans in England would suit very well. This explanation fitted oddly with Spenser's earlier contention that the inhabitants of Ireland had all fallen prey to the Scythian addiction. But more importantly for his readers, its suggestion that the Normans had imposed common law on England by force ran directly counter to the orthodox belief that in its essentials, the English constitution long pre-dated the coming of the Normans, and was merely adapted and developed by them.[32]

Spenser deepened these difficulties when he sought to face a further difficulty arising from his scheme of political reconstruction. Even if English law was indeed the most suitable law for Ireland, how could the Irish themselves be maintained in continuing allegiance to it, and prevented from sliding back to their old ways? Spenser's answer was blunt: "since we cannot now apply laws fit to the people, we will apply the people and fit them to the laws" (*View*, p. 142). This conclusion was, of course, in open contradiction to the fundamental premise on which he had launched his critique of traditional reform and thus fully undermined his argument for the necessity of the great military campaign. But what was even more disturbing was the implicit suggestion that the English law was not an organic entity that developed and expanded through the history of a community, but an artificial construct that could be imposed by power alone.

It is extremely doubtful whether Spenser intended these implications to be followed, or whether indeed he was fully conscious of their significance himself. But it is nonetheless clear that out of his critique of the failure of English rule in Ireland, there arose a series of questions concerning the essential character of the common law which neither Spenser nor his intended readers were prepared to face.

The silencing of Spenser's *View*, and his own self-censorship in abandoning the manuscript in an incomplete form, represented therefore more than a mere concession to political expediency or propagandist sensitivities, but a recognition that his way of explaining England's failure to govern Ireland was by definition untenable. The unresolved contradictions of the *View* thus marked the impasse at which the course of Tudor reform thought ended. For the remaining years of Elizabeth's reign critical commentary on England's Irish experience was displaced by simple military descriptions and, like Spenser's own "Briefe Note", unargued demands for a resort to violence.[33] It was not until the appearance of Sir John Davies's *Discovery of the True Causes Why Ireland Was Never Entirely Subdued* (1612) that a sustained analysis like Spenser's was again to be essayed. By the time Davies wrote, however, he had no need to urge a campaign of military conquest; for the suppression of the Ulster rebellion and the related uprisings in each of the provinces in the years between 1593 and 1603 had already confirmed English control in Ireland. Nor had he any need to advocate the radical measures of social and cultural reorganisation proposed by Spenser; for the common law itself, he was sure, when skillfully and forcefully applied by a determined judiciary, would be sufficient to bring about the required change. For this reason finally Davies had no cause to provide a fundamental critique of the failure of English law in Ireland such as Spenser had essayed; but could content himself with a sustained historical narrative emphasising contingency and accident and dwelling upon the errors, misjudgements and misfortunes which had prevented previous statesmen from initiating the reform that was now at last under way.[34]

Davies's recovery of these underlying themes in conventional Tudor reform thought was, of course, deceptive. His conception of the way in which the law was to be employed and of the objectives which it was to serve was far more aggressive and exploitative than that envisaged by the promoters of surrender and regrant. But his apparent espousal of the old reform assumptions served several important ideological purposes. It reaffirmed a tradition in English political thinking on Ireland and obscured thereby the disruptions, reversals and loss of confidence experienced in the previous half-century. It cloaked also the degree to which late Elizabethan writing on Ireland had departed from the canons of conventional English political thought in general. But most importantly it laid to rest the profoundly disturbing implications concerning the nature of the common-law itself raised in Spenser's agonised tract.

1. For Cowley's recommendations see *Letters and Papers of Henry VIII*, xi, 1536, no. 1049; for proposals to establish garrisons see the unsigned tract *c.* 1528 B.L. Lansdowne MS 159 no. 1 and "Report of the Irish council", 1536, *State Papers Henry VIII*, ii, pp. 409-19.
2. Printed in Walter Harris (ed.) *Hibernia* i (1747) pp. 39-52.
3. Brendan Bradshaw, *The Irish Constitutional Revolution of the Sixteenth Century* (Cambridge, 1979).
4. Report to Thomas Cromwell 1533, *State Papers Henry VIII*, ii, pp. 166-79; Opinion of John Alen, ibid., pp. 480-86.
5. Sir William Darcy, "Articles", 1515, *Calendar of Carew MSS, 1515-74*, pp. 6-8; "Report on the State of Ireland", 1515, *State Papers Henry VIII*, ii, pp. 1-31; Justice Luthrell's book, ibid., pp. 477-80.
6. See in particular Bradshaw, Ch. 2.
7. Unsigned tract, 1528, B.L. Lansdowne MS 159, no. 1; "Memo" *State Papers Henry VIII*, ii, pp. 166-79; John Alen's opinion; 1537, ibid., pp. 480-86. For the crown's formal commitment to the reform of Ireland by institutional reconstruction see "Ordinances for the Government of Ireland", 1533 *State Papers Henry VIII*, ii, pp. 107-16.
8. For a good summary of administrataive developments see Steven Ellis, *Tudor Ireland* (London, 1985), Ch. 6.
9. B.L. Lansdowne MS 159, nos. 23-24.
10. Nicholas Canny (ed.) "Rowland White's 'Discors touching Ireland' c. 1569", *Irish Historical Studies* 20 (1976-7), 451-83, and "Rowland White's 'Dysorders of the Irisshery' 1571", *Studia Hibernica* 19 (1979), 147-60.
11. Edmund Campion, *Two bokes of the historie of Ireland*, ed. A. Vossen (Assen, 1963), pp. 145-51.
12. Public Record Office (London) S.P. 63/124/24.
13. P.R.O. S.P. 63/124/24.
14. White "Dysorders of the Irisshery", pp. 157-8.
15. . For Dowdall's criticisms see P.R.O. S.P. 62/2/45; for Bermingham, P.R.O. S.P. 63/6/24, 28, 49, 53.
16. For Walshe's views see *The Office and Duety in Fighting for Our Countrey* (London, 1545); D. B. Quinn (ed.), "Conjectures on the state of Ireland, 1552", *Irish Historical*

Studies 5 (1947), 303-22; "A detection of errors" *c.* 1559, B.L. Cotton MSS Titus B XII no. 48.

17. Ciarán Brady, "Conservative subversives: the community of the Pale and the Dublin administration, 1556-1586" in P. J. Corish (ed.) *Radicals, Rebels and Establishments* (Belfast, 1986), pp. 11-32.

18. For particular expressions of Gerrard's views see "Gerrard papers", *Analecta Hibernica* 2 (1931), 93-291, especially pp. 93-101, 183-7; and his "Observations on the government of Ireland", P.R.O. S.P. 63/60/20.

19. For representative examples see Malby's reports to Walsingham, P.R.O. S.P. 63/60/37, 55, and Bingham's "Discourse", P.R.O. S.P. 63/L26/83.

20. D. B. Quinn, *The Elizabethans and the Irish* (Ithaca, 1966), especially Ch. 9; Nicholas Canny, *The Elizabethan conquest of Ireland: a pattern established, 1565-76* (Hassocks, 1976), especially Ch. 6.

21. "The evidence is admittedly scattered and no individual writer stuck consistently to one point of view" (Canny (1976), p. 131).

22. For Gilbert's views see B.L. Add. MS. 48015 ffs. 124-30, and his "Discourse on Ireland" in D. B. Quinn (ed.) *Voyages and Colonising Enterprises of Sir Humphrey Gilbert* (London, 1938-9), pp. 124-8.

23. For Perrot's views see British Library Add. Ms. 480L7, FFS. 86-90; Lambeth Palace Carew MSS. 621 for 97-115.

24. For Tremayne's views see P.R.O. S.P. 63/32/64-65 B.L. Add. MS. 48015 ff. 274-79; B.L. Cotton Titus B XII ff. 357-60.

25. See Rich's "Informations" of 1589 and 1591, P.R.O. S.P. 63/144/25; 63/158/12.

26. See Trollope's reports to Sir Francis Walsingham and Lord Burghley, 12 September 1585, 26 October 1587, P.R.O. S.P. 63/85/39; S.P. 63/131/64.

27. Ed. W. E. Buckley (London, 1887); for a further discussion of Herbert's views and his differences with Spenser see Brendan Bradshaw, "Robe and Sword in the conquest of Ireland", in Claire Cross et al (ed.) *Law and Government Under the Tudors* (Cambridge, 1988), pp. 140-52.

28. Beacon, *Solon his Follie* (Oxford, 1594); see also Bradshaw (1988), especially pp. 152-4.

29. For contrasting views on Beacon see Nicholas Canny and Ciarán Brady, "Debate: Spenser's Irish Crisis", *Past and Present* 120 (August 1988), 201-15.

30. Ciarán Brady, "Spenser's Irish Crisis: Humanism and Experience in the 1590s", *Past and Present* III (May 1986), 17-49.

31. Jonathan Goldberg, *James I and the Politics of Literature: Shakespeare, Donne and their Contemporaries* (Baltimore, 1983), pp. 9-10; David J. Baker, " 'Some quirk, some subtle evasion': Subversion in Spenser's *A View of the Present State of Ireland*", *Spenser Studies* 6 (1986), 147-163.

32. See in general, J. G. A. Pocock, *The Ancient Constitution and the Feudal Law* (Cambridge, 1957), Chs. 1-3; D. W. Hanson, *From Kingdom to Commonwealth* (Cambridge, Mass., 1970), Chs. 6-7.

33. *Works of Edmund Spenser: A Variorum Edition* (Baltimore, 1932-49), Vol. IX, pp. 244-5.

34. On Davies's conception of the nature and uses of law, see in general Hans Pawlisch, *Sir John Davies and the Conquest of Ireland* (Cambridge, 1985).

"Some secret scourge which shall by her come unto England": Ireland and Incivility in Spenser

PATRICIA COUGHLAN

I

This essay is an attempt to perceive and examine Spenser's thought about Ireland as a totality. My intention is to approach in two complementary ways the question of the meaning of Ireland in Spenser's work. In that work Ireland constitutes a radical alterity – a challenging otherness – to Spenser's consciousness, and I propose to examine the ways that alterity is registered in his writings, and the strategies they use to encounter and contain it. Ireland is a prime site of difficulty and complexity, both in its stubborn recalcitrant self, and in the dilemmas to which it gives rise in those who must have to do with it. The essay will focus particularly on two topics: first, on Spenser's various images of incivility in human behaviour and way of life, particularly those which are explicitly named as Irish, and his associated representations of the Irish landscape or territory; and second, on the significance of Spenser's use of dialogue form in *A View of the Present State of Ireland*.

My method will be to treat Spenser's writing as the site of a single complex of thought where Ireland and the Irish are concerned, differently expressed – and, indeed, variously edited and suppressed – in the poetry and the *View*, and riven by internal contradictions, but richly repaying a comparative approach seeking to comprehend the continuity of symbolic representations with social behaviour. I shall approach these writings without recognizing the conventionally observed split between Spenser's political ideology and actions on the one hand, and his cultural practice on the other – that is, between his policy proposal for the better government of Ireland, made by the Clerk to the Council of Munster and New English planter, in the form of a prose dialogue, and his courtly epic and pastoral verse. It is not that I intend to ignore the generic conventions which assuredly do differentiate these works. But it is true that until very recently analysts of the two kinds of text have continued to grant the force of a timeless and absolute division to a combined privileging of Art above Life and separation of the two originating in the nineteenth century and which would have been quite foreign to Spenser himself and to his contemporaries. As a result a division of labour was instituted in approaching the problems raised by the writings. It oversimplifies this situation only slightly to describe it as follows: historians cleaving to the *View* as to a clear window on matters of fact and politics, literary critics preserving the imaginative structures of *The Faerie Queene* supposedly immune from the infection of mere ideology, each politely acknowledging the notional integrity of the other domain, a state of affairs resulting in an impoverishment of both kinds of discussion. The work in recent years of historians such as Nicholas Canny and Ciarán Brady, and of literary scholars such as David Norbrook and Stephen Greenblatt, has greatly improved upon the earlier situation. Brady's 1986 essay on the *View*, for example, acknowledges the internal contradictions which beset it and shows a lively awareness of the necessity to pay some attention, at least, to the part played by the form of that text in determining its meaning.[1] On the one hand, texts such as the *View*, and indeed much less obviously polished and sophisticated writings, are obliged to partake just as much as does tragedy or pastoral of the communicative resources of the period – the contemporary forms of rhetoric, fictionality, and symbol. In the specific case of the *View*, the textual fact of its dialogue form has still not been sufficiently attended to; it is highly significant that for his explanation of the pitfalls of Irish government Spenser deliberately chose a genre with such strong classical and humanist associations of civility and urbane philosphical reflection. On the other hand, no magic circle exists which would cut off *The Faerie Queene* from implication in an ideological position among the discursive products of the 1590s. As Lauro Martines remarks in his discussion of the culture of the Italian city-states, there is ''no escape from the world, even in

imagined structures".[2] The myth of the gentle poet found perhaps its
most eloquent formulation in Yeats's celebrated hypothesis of the corruption, allegedly evident in the *View*, of Spenser's imagination by his
role as colonial official. But the work of Greenblatt and Norbrook has
shown clearly that this myth – the comfortable notion of a dreamy
creature of the imagination, discussable in a sphere set apart from the
iron insistences of the *View* – cannot be sustained.[3] Power and poetry are
bound up together, as Hazlitt pointed out; and far from resisting that
relation, or occasionally falling back into it in the manner of one giving
in to a temptation, Spenser constantly and expressly gestures towards a
given, ideological, truth outside the poetic work.

II

Before examining Spenser's accounts of Irish incivility, it is perhaps
necessary to remark that he did not, of course, construct these images
purely in an empirical way – out of his own actual participation in the
intensive phase of Elizabethan colonization in Ireland in the 1580s and
1590s. In his writing there is a conjunction of two sets of inherited stock
images with sixteenth-century Munster actuality in all its complexity.
What were these two sets of images – one specific to the Irish, one
general? Specifically, a large stock of fixed representations of the Irish
already existed, constructed during the centuries-long interaction of prejudice and experience in the power relations of Irish and English. It will
not be appropriate here to detail the features of these stereotypes, freshly
deployed from standard sources like Giraldus Cambrensis by Elizabethan
writers such as Camden, a specific influence on Spenser; Joseph
Leerssen's recent *Mere Irish and Fior-Ghael* provides a very full account
of the matter.[4] But more generally, Spenser's images of the Irish were
also most assuredly formed by his intellectual and emotional familiarity
with the Renaissance Christian typology of the wildness outside civil
society. This set of representations has been well described by Hayden
White, and one may form an impression of its interweaving with and
modification by actual colonial activities by bringing general theoretical
discussions such as White's into relation with specific case-histories of
the various colonial fields, such as D. B. Quinn's on the Irish, James
Muldoon's on the North American Indians, Peter Hulme's on the Caribbean, and Anthony Pagden's analysis of Spanish interpretations of
South American indigenes in the context of their rule over them.[5] In spite

of the major actual differences between these various places and people, their colonizing interpreters came to them equipped with more or less the same model of civility *versus* barbarity, formed in the tradition of European classical and Christian thought.

In the discussion which follows I shall be mainly considering Spenser's images specifically of the "wild", or native, Irish, and paying less attention to his attacks on the Old English, the largely Catholic descendants of earlier English arrivals, of whose part-assimilation to the native culture he so strongly disapproved. One should, however, remark Spenser's evident intention to blur for his mainland readers the actual distinctions between the two groups, and his extensive use of the *topos* of the degeneration of the Old English to tar both with the same brush. The merging of the two kinds of figure – wild man by origin, and degenerate – is, as we shall see, interestingly evident on occasion in *The Faerie Queene.*[6]

It will be useful to pause on White's description of the complex of Renaissance beliefs about barbarians and Wild Men, figures distinguishable, but nevertheless often merged. He describes the Wild Man – believed to dwell on the fringes of civil society, in mountain wastes, forests and caves – as a figure primarily inspiring fear and disgust, in two different ways:

> the Wild Men represented a threat to the individual, both as nemesis and as a possible destiny, both as enemy and as representative of a condition into which an individual man, having fallen out of grace or having been driven from his city, might degenerate.[7]

The Wild Man was often portrayed as dumb or a meaningless babbler, thus as lacking the most essential qualification for civility, language. Further, existing outside the city, the necessary locus for the achievement of civility or full human function, both barbarians and Wild Men were conceived, following classical and medieval writers, as being enslaved to nature and unable to control their passions; they were characterized as

> mobile, shifting, confused, chaotic . . . incapable of sedentary existence, of self-discipline, and of sustained labour . . .[8]

Wildness was understood rather as a lack, a failure to realize full human potentiality, than as a positive force; the Wild Man represents the deeply threatening image of the man outside social control, "the man in whom the libidinal impulses have gained full ascendancy". White finds that a transformation of this strongly negative representation into a positive image connoting desirable freedom and natural innocence, a proto-Noble Savage figure, takes place in the fourteenth and fifteenth centuries, and indeed, following Richard Bernheimer's study of wildness as a medieval literary topic, points to an instance in Spenser himself of such a gentle savage. As we shall see, however, it is negative and deeply anxious and hostile versions of "salvage" men which in fact predominate in Spenser's work; the benign Wild Man is fairly exceptional.[9] In most cases his subhuman otherness is a matter for detestation and fear. But this is not a simple matter: bearing in mind the prevailing fixed convictions about the incivility of those without a native urban culture, still in Spenser's attitude to Ireland and the Irish there is a marked uncertainty of perspective, a series of complex contradictions and tensions. I shall argue in the second section of this essay that these tensions are also manifest in the dialogical form of the *View*, in ways which have not been adequately explored.

Let us consider the range of Spenser's representations of Wild Man figures in his work and investigate the relation of these figures to his reaction of disgust at and hostility chiefly towards the native Irish. Both the *View* and *The Faerie Queene* construct descriptions of barbarous persons and groups, who are *either* completely incapable of civility, *or* ultimately redeemable, but not yet rendered civil by submission to good order. Both texts explore in a deeply troubled manner the tension beween these two versions of "salvage" men and nations; and in both, though the question is not absolutely decided, there is a strong tendency to conclude that civility cannot be easily or promptly learned, and that only the eradication of such barbarous creatures will answer. Discussing the ideology of colonization, Nicholas Canny indentifies in Elizabethan colonial discussions at large a progressive hardening of the assumption that on the nature either of the Gaelic Irish or the American Indian, "nurture will never stick", and that extirpation, or at the very least bloody campaigns of reduction, is the right approach.[10] The more optimistic view, that such peoples *were* capable of becoming civil and, subsequently, Christian subjects, was to be found in Elizabethan Ireland, but rather among the old English, who were in Spenser's eyes themselves contaminated by their too complete participation in Irish culture.[11] Nevertheless, it is striking that there are moments, especially in *The Faerie Queene*, when he does invent some "salvage wights" about whose development to fully human status he can express a sense of possibility.

An example of such moments is the saving of Una in Book I.vi from Sansloy, who is about to rape her, by a "salvage nation", who, though they look repulsive – "a rude, misshapen, monstrous rablement" – do comfort and pity her. Una is at first afraid to commit "her single person to their barbarous truth" but then recognizes their basically benign nature. They honour her, crown her and try to worship her (I.vi.11ff.). So remote are they from Christian undertanding that when she discourages them from this they turn instead to adoring her donkey. This has its parallel in the *View*, in the inadequate grasp of Christianity attributed to the Catholic Irish:

> . . . the most of the Irish are so far from understanding of the popish religion as they are of the protestants' profession. (*View*, p. 161)

We may discern here the horrified reactions of Protestant Englishmen to the Gaelic Irish practice of Catholicism – more outlandish and distasteful even than the "normal", Anglicized version prevailing in the Pale.[12] The episode of Una's faun and satyr rescuers suggests, however, that natural man *can* live well even in his unregenerate state (the salvage nation's behaviour compares favourably with that of the rapacious Sansloy), and further that the forest can be made the setting for religious enlighten- ment, at least to some degree. In the *View*, too, though very rarely, there are moments of optimism, when it is felt that the mere Irish can be drawn from "the former rudeness in which they were bred" by the wonderful power of learning which "can soften and temper the most stern and salvage nature" (p. 159). In *The Faerie Queene*, VI.iv.4ff., there is another benign "salvage man" who saves the lady Serena and her inade- quate knight Calepine from the evil Turpine. He is "naked, without needful vestiments", has no armour or knightly weapons, and lacks articulate language. He is also immune to the fear of attack, and magically invulnerable. Serena at first fears this natural creature, but unnecessarily, because as it turns out he respects and admires her – out of an innate goodness, it is explained. He lives deep in the forest, without roof or bedding, and neither tills the soil, nor eats any meat, living on "the frutes of the forrest", which makes him a "bad Stuard" in the nar- rator's eyes. This "salvage man" in VI is, however, different from those in I, in that it is stressed that he is a degenerate, someone who has once had, but has lost, the attributes of civility, rather than an ineffable primitive. It is odd and interesting that Spenser should treat such a character so favourably; when the characteristics used to describe him turn up again in the *View*, they have invariably a sharply negative tone. It has not been sufficiently noticed that this "salvage man" is in fact a compound of characteristics which are distributed, in the *View*, between Gaelic Irish and Old English. The latter are in Spenser's eyes examples of degeneracy: he makes the English spokesman Eudoxus express sorrowing wonder that they can have sunk into such a "Lethargie" that they have "even forgotten their English names" (p. 115). Yet the "gently born" salvage man in *The Faerie Queene* VI who has lost not only his name but even the faculty of using human language is presented as benign, revealing the capacity of Spenser's consciously fictive work to idealize characteristics which could not on the literal level be approved: a process we shall encounter again in discussing the *Mutabilitie Cantos*.

Failure to plough, sow, or eat red meat, are characteristics attributed in the *View* to the Irish, who are said to live on "white meats" (curds) and milk; and the *View* also inveighs famously against the "barbarous" use of their mantles as bedding and shelter by the Irish rebels and herdsmen (pp. 51-2). These points loom large in Spenser's attack on Gaelic Irish culture. Of course the practice of "booleying" or transhumance – seasonal movement between lower and higher pastures – and the strongly pastoral character of Irish agriculture in general drew a hostile reaction from many of the Elizabethan colonists.[13] Such a shifting population with its large numbers of apparently "idle" cowherds and "horseboys", made in Spenser's and other English eyes for insecurity and offered cover to the warrior class of remoter districts. (We may recall White's characterization of the Wild Man as unstable, chaotic, shifting, and incapable of sedentary life.) The pastoral way of life can evidently figure as an ideal only within the conventions of poetry; the actual Irish cattle-based version posed too many problems. (In *The Faerie Queene* VI.x.35 and 37 Spenser revealingly derives "coward" from "cowherd".) The booleying reminded the English planters and officials of central Asian and other barbarian nomadic practices, usually labelled "Scythian". So

> unto the plough therefore are all those loose stocaghs and horseboys to be driven, and made to employ that ableness of body which they were wonte to use to theft and villainy henceforth to labour and husbandry . . . (*View*, p. 157)

Throughout the *View* there is a set of antitheses between ideas of looseness, wildness, wandering, illicit liberty, on the one hand, and of control, order, and repression on the other: between the Irish, who "swerve", "straggle", "miche in corners", "break forth", "walk disorderly", are "loose", "wandering", "idly roguing", "loitering", and the policy to be used to "let them have the bitterness of martial law", to have them "shortly to be brought in by the ears", "tythed and bound" to a particular place, "particularly entered and set down in the tything books", and so forth.[14] Like the wild villainous characters in *The Faerie Queene*, the Irish are a "rebellious rout of loose people . . . infesting the woods and spoiling the good subject".[15]

Turning now from the inhabitants to the actual terrain of Ireland, one finds that in Spenser it also wears two faces. Sometimes its fertility and potential for development are praised, in the manner of contemporary advertisements for planters such as that of Robert Payne, but more forceful by far is its negative face: it is mostly composed of dark and impenetrable forests, mountains and bogs, threatening places among which a savage and implacable enemy fleetingly appears and disappears; as the *View* has it:

> he is a flying enemy, hiding himself in woods and bogs, from where he will not draw forth but into some strait passage or perilous ford where he knows the army must needs pass, there he will lie in wait . . . (*View*, p. 98)

Irenius outlines a "plot" for the rendering harmless of this landscape, by shutting down and containing it in "streight passages and strong enclosures". The forests are to be removed:

> first I wish that order were taken for the cutting down and opening of all paces through woods, so that a wide space of a hundred yards might be laid open in every of them for the safety of travellers . . . (*View*, p. 164)

He plans to have "bridges built" on all the rivers, and "all the fords marred and spilt so that none might pass any other ways but by those bridges"; and to fortify all the "passages between two Bogs". He would set a governor at Athlone (guarding the main route out of Connacht) "upon the skirts of that unquiet country"; and ultimately the land is to be "enclosed and well fenced" (pp. 164, 83). As Michael McCarthy-Morrogh shows in his study of the Munster plantation, travel outside towns in this period was indeed made sufficiently difficult by the lack of bridges and roads, even without the additional risk of hostile encounters.[16]

To the seething violence of this countryside in Spenser's account of it, an equal violence of repression must be brought: a relentless winter pursuit of the enemy which will reduce him to starvation and therefore to submission:

> It is not with Ireland as with other countries, where the wars flame most in summer, and the helmets glister brightest in the fair sunshine, but in Ireland the winter yieldeth best services, for then the trees are bare and naked, which use both to clothe and hide the kern, the ground is cold and wet which useth to be his bedding, the air is sharp and bitter to blow through his naked sides and legs, the kine are barren and without milk which useth to be his onely food; neither if he kill them, then will they yield him flesh, nor if he keep them will they give him food, besides then being all in calf, for the most part they will through much chasing and driving, cast all their calves and lose all their milk which should relieve him the next summer after. (*View*, pp. 100-1)

It will be recalled that throughout *The Faerie Queene*, brightly shining armour and weaponry are the signs of the good knight's active virtue.[17] But in the *View* the description of such fit and proper war accoutrements is merely an instant of beauty and pleasure; the place where "the wars flame most in summer and the helmets glister brightest in the fair sunshine" is somewhere else, the shining moment of chivalric clarity is quickly past, and the inhuman plan of hunting down the kerns like their cattle takes its place. Yet the harshness of their fate is not spared in the language: "the air is sharp and bitter to blow through his naked sides". The paragraph yokes together the two moments, of glamour and ruthlessness, almost casually. Here again is the tension between the rebel as enemy and as victim; it is not permitted to amount to a contradiction. But just as in *The Faerie Queene* the possible goodness of natural man is sometimes entertained, so the *View* has some moments in which pity for the Irish does seem to supplant rage, fear and disgust. Alienation from them and the intense sense of their otherness are replaced by a momentarily vivid awareness of them as kindred flesh. Such moments occur particularly in the well-known passages in which Irenius recounts his memories of the famine following the Desmond Rebellion in the 1580s. He grants that there may actually be some Irish – "old men, women, children and hinds" – who did not partake in the rising, and who when they are turned away by the rebels, "though policy would turn them back again . . . yet in a pitiful commiseration I would wish them to be received" (p. 102). "A pitiful commiseration" presumes the sense of a common humanity with the object of pity, the turning in fact of such people into feeling subjects and thus creatures not absolutely other. After a year and a half of rebellion, says Irenius,

> they were brought to such wretchedness, as that any stony heart would have rued the same. Out of every corner of the woods and glens they came creeping forth upon their hands, for their legs could not bear them. They looked anatomies of death, they spake like ghosts crying out of their graves, they did eat the dead carrions, happy where they could find them, yea and one another soon after in so much as the very carcasses they spared not to scrape out of their graves . . . (*View*, p. 104)

"Any stony heart would have rued the same"; but the memory of such "rue" does not prevent Irenius' advocacy now of a scorched-earth policy, which is clearly intended to produce the same effects. Just a little earlier in the dialogue, he has assured Eudoxus that "one winter's well following" of the kern "will so pluck him on his knees that he will never be able to stand up again".

Finally, let us look at the most clearly positive aspect of Spenser's representations of Ireland: the landscape idealized, as it is sometimes rendered in *The Faerie Queene*. In the poem, as opposed to the dialogue, though there sometimes *are* incursions from the wilds upon the settled subjects – for instance in the attack on the house of Alma in II.ix – more usually the Irish countryside is appropriated benignly, made to function in a mythopoeic process. Such passages reconstruct it as an ideal territory, to which the beauty of perfect order is imputed by the genial personification of Munster mountains and streams. The river-marriage episode in IV.xi uses the attendance of the Irish rivers in a general British procession to prefigure optimistically the acquiescence, in fact withheld, of the inhabitants in the conquest and plantation. More interesting is the deployment of topography in the Mutabilitie Cantos at the end of the poem, because there a resistance to any such facile resolution is registered. The main topic of the Cantos is the rebellion of Mutabilitie against Jove and its containment by decree alone; there is also a secondary episode, the Faunus-Diana story (vi.38-55), and both are of importance to this discussion.

In this minor tale, which is enclosed by the major one, Faunus is a wood-god, who hides, like the Irish rebels, in a thicket; but unlike them he does it for a voyeur's reason. Diana and her attendants haul him out "into the open light", and consider castrating him, but decide against it, because it is necessary that wood-gods should continue to exist as a species; instead they dress him in animal-skins and hunt him to exhaustion. All of this is of course impeccably Ovidian, but to the reader of the *View* it cannot fail to have also strong echoes of Irenius' policy programme for Ireland. At the end of the episode Diana's anger causes her to curse the whole district of "faire forests" and "richest champaign", to the effect

> . . . that Wolves where she was wont to space,
> Should harbour'd be, and all those Woods deface,
> And Thieves should rob and spoile that Coast around.
> Since which, those Woods, and all that goodly Chase,
> Doth to this day with Wolves and Thieves abound:
> Which too-too true that lands in-dwellers since have found.
>
> (VII.vi.44-5)

The whole story might be read as a minor mythic transformation of Irish actuality in the 1590s, a dream re-enactment with the harm removed and a magical or metaphysical reason provided for the infestation of the Munster surroundings with dread and horror; a revision of history which eliminates the "anatomies of death". One might also notice that by this explanation, the Irish landscape becomes not the *original* haunt of barbarity and incivility, but a place which has degenerated from a former state of order, and, we may conclude, on those grounds a less hopeless place. This relinquishing of the actual for a passage to a metaphysical level undermines the general sense of a retreat from active intervention in the world which has often been noticed about the latter part of *The Faerie Queene*.

As Brady puts it:

The principal subject [in Book VI and the Mutabilitie Cantos] is the means by which the good man may come to terms with and make his peace in a world he cannot control.[18]

As has often been pointed out, the rebellion of Mutabilitie against Jove is also full of echoes of Spenser's explicitly Irish discussions. Mutabilitie is a "rebel", of the stock of the Titans, whose rule was usurped, in Greek mythology, by Jove. She is "bred of that bad seed"; she intends, as Jove says, to thrust

. . . our selves from heavens high Empire,
    If that her might were match to her desire. (VII.vi.21)

Mutabilitie, for her part, argues that she represents the rightful succession. Jove insists that the power is his for two reasons: the right of conquest and "the eternall doome of Fates decree" (VII.vi.33). The insistence on the rights of conquest is one frequently resorted to by Elizabethan writers on Ireland as part of a legalistic justification of English rule; the other reason Jove gives, the decree of fate, might be interpreted both as a characteristically Protestant invocation of divine providence, and as a pragmatic, not to say cynical, argument. The character and role of Mutabilitie in the poem certainly have much in common with Spenser's characterization of the Irish of various complexions: she shows incurable restlessness and a recalcitrance to reforming efforts, and is above all a force for disturbance in the world. Her defence is to appeal over the head of Jove to a higher court, that of Nature; a gesture which suggests a further parallel between Mutabilitie's role and that of the Irish, who as we have seen are required by colonial ideology to be portrayed as merely natural, or at best semi-civilized, creatures. Spenser critics have found a "contradiction" in Mutabilitie's plea: as A. C. Hamilton puts it, "a rebel cannot go to court to defend rebellion".[19] But Mutabilitie is here engaging in a procedure very commonly adopted by Old English magnates (and sometimes by native ones) in sixteenth- and even seventeenth-century Ireland, namely, going above the heads of the Dublin administrators and using their direct links with the monarch to bring about their policy demands against Dublin orders.[20]

Earlier, in his pastoral poem *Colin Clouts Come Home Againe*, written in 1591, Spenser had attempted to combine both aspects of his vision of Ireland; but the result is uneasily paradoxical and confusing, and strains the pastoral form of the poem. On the one hand, he adopts the fiction of making Munster the native place of his persona Colin Clout, both the "home" of the title and an enchanting pastoral landscape in which he traces a topographical myth of river-courtships (the loves of the Mulla and Bregog streams). On the other hand, Ireland is described as "that desert", and as "that waste, where I was quite forgot" (recalling the language of the *View*, which represents Ireland as consisting of "great mountains and waste deserts full of grass").[21] It is contrasted sharply with the peace and plenty of distant England, where there is "no wayling" nor "wretchednesse":

> No griesly famine, nor no raging sweard,
> No nightly bodrags, nor no hue and cries;
> The shepheards there abroad may safely lie,
> On hills and downes, withouten dread or daunger:
> No ravenous wolves the good mans hope destroy,
> Nor outlawes fell affray the forest raunger. (ll. 308-19)

One may well ask, as Colin's listener does:

> Why didst thou ever leave that happie place,
> In which such wealth might unto thee accrew?
> And back returnedst to this barrein soyle,
> Where cold and care and penury do dwell:
> Here to keep sheepe, with hunger and with toyle . . . (ll. 654-8)

But for answer the poem provides only an admission of incomprehension, or at least of incapacity to make sense of Colin's situation: "Most wretched he, that is and cannot tell" (l. 659). Colin has somehow *both* willingly opted for his outcast state – he "rather chose back to his sheep to turne" (l. 672) – *and* been cast out without his volition, there being no place at court, as he puts it, for "gentle wit", "single truth", or "simple honestie" (ll. 708, 727) – or in other words for such a trenchant critic of court lewdness and venality. Colin says he has chosen exile as a matter of principle, but chafes at this state; and the place which he presents himself as having chosen to leave is both desirable and fallen. With a similar and matching uncertainty of perspective, Ireland too is contradictory: it is simultaneously a beautiful, fertile, fictionally native land, and a "waste desert" full of human and inhuman horrors. Thus both the directions in which he can turn are fraught with negatives. We shall encounter this situation again, differently framed but quite recognizable, in examining the dialogical mode of existence of the *View*.

III

As I have remarked at the outset of this discussion, it has until recently been usual among commentators on Spenser to treat fairly cursorily the fact that the *View* is a dialogue, as if the work were simply an expository one, fairly plain and transparent as to language and form. I propose to argue here that the dialogue form of the *View* deserves to be treated as far from a mere polite learned surface, and to explore how revealing this form is of the characteristic tensions in Spenser's thought and position which we have just been examining largely on the level of content, in the discussion of his versions of Irish recalcitrance and otherness both human and territorial.

To explore Spenser's employment of this form, it will be useful to examine its generic character.[22] The Renaissance dialogue form was the inheritor of the Platonic and Ciceronian practice of philosophical debate and the product of the humanist social milieu of oligarchies and courts. It is the generic embodiment of civility – in the case of the *View*, itself an instance of that civility whose lack in Ireland it inveighs against. The likes of Spenser and his fellow official in Munster, Richard Beacon, also the author of a political dialogue about Ireland, wrote against the background of a rich formal tradition, both from the Renaissance and from antiquity, in English, Greek, Latin and other European languages. In the modern period, dialogue had ranged from Reformation religious polemic, in the hands of Thomas More and his Protestant opponents, to genial reflection on manners and morals in Erasmus's *Colloquies* – used far and wide as a grammar school textbook – and the urbane courtesy handbooks and high neo-Platonic reflection of the Italian humanists. Furthermore, the dialogical construction of thought was a scholastic habit deeply ingrained from both grammar-school and university curricula, in which the holding of formal disputations survived as a common pedagogical exercise, in spite of some modern attacks on such scholastic set practices.[23]

Two main kinds of dialogue are normally defined, from antiquity on: one, the Platonic, which is much the rarer, is genuinely an encounter between opposing views and a real rehearsal of their confrontation; the other, the Ciceronian or expository dialogue, more common, merely sets out, with maximum courtesy and clarity, the correct attitude to an outlined issue. Formally, both kinds make an implicit claim to openness and geniality, to represent a consensus in whatever conclusions are arrived at, and to arrive at those conclusions by the exercise of a rationality which can tolerate the expression of opposing views; they pretend to thrash the matter out without the blatant suppression of the dissenting voice. But not all even of Socrates's own dialogues are Platonic in the sense I have outlined above; when they are, a genuine struggle is enacted – ultimately, as Erich Voegelin argues, the struggle between Socrates and Athens, which was won historically by Athens, but philosophically and imaginatively by Socrates:

> [Plato's] desire was to show the philosopher in the dramatic instant of seeking and finding, and to make the doubt and conflict visible.[24]

Socrates will not entertain fake contributions to the argument; he insists, for example, that the Sophists should not get away with long rhetorical harangues, however elegant, but must address the issue.

Predominant Renaissance versions of the form are mostly much nearer to Cicero, who offers genial expositions of mainstream philosophy: a map rather than an act of discovery. As Roger Deakins remarks,

> Dialogue, since Agricola, has been committed to "informing" rather than to a give-and-take of genuinely opposed points of view.[25]

Studies prescriptive and descriptive of the art of dialogue and the nature of dialectic multiplied in the course of the sixteenth century, as the work of Deakins and C. J. R. Armstrong has recently shown. Armstrong finds a strain of what he calls "probabilism" in the contribution of some of the great humanist writers – Vives, Sturm, Ramus – to the composition of dialogue and the art of argument in it:

> This dialectic . . . concerned . . . with greater and less probability was decidedly not conceived as delivering "answers" in the way that a well-conducted piece of algebraic reasoning delivers the values of x, y and z. It is no longer a closed system, the yardstick of true and false, but subordinate, relative.[26]

But such openness was untypical; there was a movement in the later part of the century, also noticed by Deakins in English dialogue, to resist probabilism in the interest of sternly reasserting the non-plurality of truth. So Renaissance dialogue has more in common with Socrates's opponents, the Sophists, than with Socrates himself. In this connection Stephen Greenblatt's observation that in Renaissance writing

> Socrates is absorbed into the ethos of rhetorical self-fashioning that Plato, in *Theaetetus* and *Gorgias*, has him condemn

is particularly useful.[27] In a discussion of Spenser, whose obsequious attitude to the queen elicited a particularly harsh condemnatory epithet from Marx, it is relevant to notice that this marks a rearrangement in the relations between the philosopher-intellectual and the state. In the Renaissance the equivalent of Athens, or the state, generally has the services of the Socrates-figures; as Lauro Martines says about the humanist historians even of republican Italian cities:

> All humanists, whatever their stripe, made a candid alliance with power. They plumped for the ruling classes, empires, and luminaries of past civil times; they also wrote in unashamed praise of their own cities, rulers and patrons.[28]

However, Renaissance versions of dialogue certainly sought to arrogate to themselves the Platonic prestige of this "symbolic form of the order of wisdom"; like dozens of other examples, the *View* is, though it is at several removes from the early humanist moment, an instance of that intention. Of course the utter difference in the social context alters the effect of the use of any form, whatever the individual intentions of a writer: the *agon* of Socrates with Athens has certainly undergone a peculiar transformation when it assumes the shape of the Munster officials proposing pragmatic colonial policies to the reluctant monarch.

But in late antiquity there also arose another kind of dialogue, that of Lucian, the second-century A.D. Greek writer from Samosata. Lucian's work merges the dialogue form with more frankly fictive genres, such as the imaginary or otherworld journey, and the description of the ideal state. Lucian is mentioned prominently in the *View*, and this is surprising, because of the irreverent, humorous character of much of his writing. His dialogues are playful, humorous, parodic and sometimes bawdy; they frequently poke fun at the pretensions of philosophers and at the gods, and are far closer in spirit to Petronius's *Satyricon* than to Plato's *Symposium*. Given to travesty, impious and cynical, Lucian is at times the most dialogical of writers (in the sense of that word developed by Mikhail Bakhtin).[29] Euphrates in what is now Turkey, was a babel of different languages: the inhabitants commonly spoke Aramaic, the educated classes operated in Greek, and the administrative language was Latin. As Bakhtin says:

> Lucian's cultural and linguistic consciousness was born and shaped at this point of intersection of cultures and languages.

Bakhtin also stresses Lucian's invocation of the

> private, everyday sphere, where one finds food, drink, sexual relations . . . in all its specificity as low and private life

and says Lucian needs this sphere "to undercut the lofty planes of ideology, which have become rigid and false".[30] By contrast Spenser is the most monological of writers: that is, he is strongly insistent upon the existence of a single authoritative order in the political and social world, and upon the necessity of repressing any dissenting voices, whose very existence is seen as dangerously threatening. As Stephen Greenblatt puts it, even in his poetry he constantly gestures beyond the frame of the fiction towards a truth given outside it. And further, Lucian's pleasure in and attention to materiality is utterly at odds with Spenser's attitude to it. Throughout *The Faerie Queene* he consistently presents physical actuality as inferior, illusory in the Platonic sense, and as the locus of dangerous temptation. His imaginative enterprise is opposite to that of Lucian (as Bakhtin characterizes it): it is a transcendence of the actual, which is seen as *merely* so, in favour of an ideal order. The great problem, and for many readers the greatest interest, of his work resides in the appalling difficulty he finds in achieving such a transcendence, and the complexity with which it is necessary to construct it imaginatively; and, as I have said, Ireland functions in his work as a major site of that difficulty and complexity.

For the reasons I have been outlining, one would not, then, be tempted to think of the *View* as dialogical in the Bakhtinian sense of authentically giving representation to a radical alterity, and Lucian seems an unlikely influence upon Spenser; but nevertheless there is interesting evidence both of his appreciation of Lucian in a general way, and of the presence of a specific Lucian text in his mind while composing the *View*. In December 1578 he arranged with his friend Gabriel Harvey that Harvey would pass him his own copy of Lucian (in four volumes) as part of a game of literary forfeits, unless Spenser had read a certain four light humorous tales (including the Spanish picaresque novel *Lazarillo* and a version of *Till Eulenspiegel*). It seems that in the event Harvey retained the Lucian. But from this we can gather that Lucian was considered frivolous but not unworthy reading. He was sometimes used as a texbook in the Renaissance and Harvey, writing to Spenser in 1580, playfully lists him as rather tending to displace more serious authors:

. . . Tully and Demosthenes nothing so much studied, as they were wonte: Livie, and Sallust possiblye rather more than lesse: Lucian never so much: Aristotle much named, but little read: Xenophon and Plato reckoned much among Discoursers, and conceited Superficiall fellowes . . .[31]

Lucian's work, however, is varied, and not all of it is blatantly anti-authoritarian; his specific presence in the *View* is in a particularly inoffensive form, as the author of the *Toxaris*, a dialogue between a Greek and a Scythian about friendship. This text, considered "an oddity among Lucian's works" because of the uncharacteristic seriousness of its tone, is especially unthreatening to Spenser's ideological position: its twin accounts of loyal and courageous friendship could easily be taken up into the Renaissance discourse of courtly behaviour, and its interest in the details of Scythian custom sanctioned and therefore neutralized as learned ethnographic enquiry (as indeed Irenius's accounts of Irish customs partly are).[32] The *Toxaris* is mentioned in the context of Irenius's general ethnohistorical speculation about the origins of the Irish. His chief candidates for the ancestry of the Irish are the Scythians. (This idea of Scythian descent is not, of course, peculiar to Spenser; it is also to be found in the work of Camden, on which he drew.) The relevant passage in the *View* is:

And by the same reason may I as reasonably conclude that the Irish are descended from the Scythians, for that they use even to this day some of the same ceremonies which the Scythians anciently used, as

for example ye may read in Lucian in that sweet dialogue which is
entitled Toxaris, or of Friendship . . . (*View*, p. 58)

and he goes on to find certain Scythian and Irish customs in common:
ways of swearing oaths, by the sword and by the fire, and ways of cook-
ing, for example seething meat over the fire in the hide of an animal.

The *Toxaris* was a famous formal model in the Renaissance: Erasmus
and Thomas More both practised their Greek and their literary skills in
making Latin versions of it.[33] The dialogue is between the charcters Toxaris and Mnesippus. Toxaris is a Scythian, Mnesippus a Greek, and the
subject of their talk is friendship. Each vies with the other in claiming
superiority for his own nation's practice of friendship, and to prove his
claim, each tells several anecdotes. At first glance it seems that this text's
detailed, if somewhat lurid, descriptions of Scythian social life account
entirely for its presence in the background of the *View*. But I wish to
argue that it is not merely this anthropological material about Scythian
customs which influenced Spenser, as has been hitherto assumed. Rather,
much more importantly, the notion of the ethnically based opposition
between two sets of values, and the nature of those values themselves,
both find striking parallels in the *View*. Secondly, Spenser obviously also
takes aesthetic pleasure in the *Toxaris* as a text, calling it "that Sweet
dialogue", which should draw our attention to its operation as a formal
parallel behind the *View* and cause us to examine comparatively the manner of the interplay between the interlocutors, as rhetorical and fictional
constructs, in both texts. A greater understanding of the use Spenser
made of the *Toxaris* should result from investigation of these two questions, and can in various ways assist the interpretation of the *View*.

Mnesippus, the Greek representative, is dry, witty and affectionately
ironic in his responses to Toxaris; he teases him with accusations of pro-
lixity, and Toxaris in turn complains that he interrupts (as Irenius does
to Eudoxus in the *View*). Mnesippus further has an attitude of disbelief
in some of the Scythian stories, which, he says, are "quite like fables".
We may compare with this Eudoxus's scepticism about Irenius's finding
the Irish bards and chronicles fit sources of historical knowledge. In
general Mnesippus stands for a norm of civility, and Toxaris is something of a wild man, only less savage than the semi-nomadic pastoral barbarians at home, whose representative he is. He refers to having left
home out of a desire for Greek culture.[34] One should note his suggestive
similarity, in this, to Spenser's pastoral persona Colin Clout, who claims

in the poem *Colin Clouts Come Home Againe* to be a rude and simple native of Ireland, to whom the sea, and still more the court, when he visits it, are strange. Kilcolman is designated "home", and the poem is presented as written from there: "From my house at Kilcolman, the 27. of December. 1591". In Lucian, Toxaris is evidently to be conceived as in part assimilated to Greek "civil conversation", as Spenser might have put it. But at the end, though a continuing friendship is being sworn between the two, Mnesippus again defines a sharp opposition between their behaviour: instead of drinking a cup of blood together to seal their bond, he says, they will simply agree verbally. He thus opposes rational resolution to participatory and physically based ritual, conversation and similarity of ideals to the shared cup of blood; the adoption of Mnesippus's suggestions at the end duly marks the hegemony of Greek over Scythian. Metropolitan culture thus remains the only conceivable ground for the operation of civilized consciousness, as is the case, implicitly, in the *View*. (This is a resolution unusual in Lucian, but normal in Spenser.) But, preserving the parallel (one presumes that about Scythians Lucian did not feel so very strongly either way), we should notice that structurally, in place of Lucian's matched tales of friendship, Spenser gives his plans for conquest, starvation, and expropriation.

How does all this illuminate the *View*? It is clear that Spenser conceived Eudoxus as, like Mnesippus, the representative of central order, the modern equivalent of Athenian culture in the ancient world; is it not also likely that at least in part he was casting his Irenius in the pendent role of a rather wild and rough character, like Toxaris? In Irenius's manner of arguing, we certainly find a passion, even sometimes a ferocity, which is drily noted and ironically soothed by Eudoxus. This immoderate quality of Irenius's and its significance may best be explained by turning to the second of our two topics for investigation in this section, the roles of the two characters in the discussion and the nature and meaning of their interplay.

One cannot say too emphatically that what enables Eudoxus and Irenius to be the means of conveying policy arguments and positions to possible readers of the text, and to represent the two sides of an *interior* debate Spenser is conducting with himself, is their prior existence as fictions, what one might call their textuality. Too little attention has customarily been given by students of the *View* either to the rhetorical moves made by the two speakers, or to what may be called their dramatic characterization, which is the product of those moves. It is true that the

View lacks dialogicality in the sense of making two different registers of language confront each other. Both voices are, linguistically speaking, equally authoritative; both are standard users of official English; neither is lexically or syntactically a less than adequate formulator of judgement or description. But this should not warrant any rash decision to write off the dialogue form, or assume it merely a decoy or mantle to conceal an absolute decisiveness.[35] As David J. Baker has recently put it:

> Irenius is not Spenser's spokesman in a simple sense, but one voice in a dialectic Spenser constructs between inadmissible scepticism of royal policy and articulations of the official "view", articulations Spenser usually puts in the mouth of Eudoxus.[36]

What kind of total impression does this interplay produce? A discourse expressly constructed as a dialogue lays particular stress on the dual character of all thought as it is analysed in the linguistic and literary work of Bakhtin's school – the constitution of both inner and outer speech, as Voloshinov describes it, by two basic tendencies, described as commentary and retort.[37] How far, then, does this duality go to constitute Eudoxus as genuinely representing an alterity to Irenius?

Firstly, within the shared standard language of the two, real differences of opinion are framed: one clear instance of such a difference is in the debate near the beginning of the *View* about whether laws can be one and universal, or need to be differently framed for different places.[38] Another is the question whether the Irish chronicles and bards' accounts of history are at all reliable. Here Eudoxus takes a standard humanist view – that they are all "fabulous and forged" – whereas Irenius insists that they *can* be used as sources.[39] Both of these are fairly important points, in an English discussion about the treatment of Ireland; as is shown by such substantial disagreements as these and others (for example the major clash about the role of "the sword"), Eudoxus *is* fashioned to provide in several respects a genuine alternative to Irenius; and it is by no means the case that the reader is successfully manipulated always to agree with the latter. Certainly Irenius is the dominant speaker, in the sense that (especially towards the end) he gets a good deal more space; nevertheless the reader has the distinct impression that Eudoxus is the one who will judge, the voice of an ultimate authority and of a knowledge not experientially derived, as Irenius's is, but given. What gives us this idea? It runs counter to the contemporary rules for disputations, as laid down by one of the standard treatises on the subject, Sigonio's *De Dialogo* (1562).[40] In his analysis of Tudor dialogue Roger Deakins finds that one of the following basic pairs of functions always underlies a superficial diversity of roles: those of Master and Pupil, Objector and Answerer; in this case the Answerer does not always satisfactorily dismiss the Objector's objections.[41] It follows that *Spenser's* attitude to the Irish issues, as distinct from Irenius's, is a complex and ambivalent one, capable at the very least of framing convincingly the likely arguments of those nearer the cultural and political centre, the capital and the court.

Secondly, discussing Eudoxus as an equivalent of Lucian's Mnesippus, I have already noted how the content of his speeches defines his role as the representative of a centralized, metropolitan, distanced viewpoint; but so too does what we may call their dramatic form. Eudoxus has often a slightly patronizing air, as of an older or more eminent man – as when he gives Irenius his head to "follow the course which you have purposed to yourself" (p. 21), or when he commends Irenius's arguments rather loftily, in a "my dear boy" tone. He is the one who constantly reminds Irenius (and the reader) of the state of the discussion and the general structure of the argument being pursued; this, like the tone Mnesippus takes with Toxaris in Lucian, is sometimes made the source of mild comedy, and has the effect of strengthening the reader's impression of a slightly disordered or frenetic quality in Irenius. The occasion of this humour is partly the defensiveness of Irenius, as if he is aware of his own over-enthusiasm; when Eudoxus asks him whether there ever were Irish High Kings, for instance, he replies:

> I would tell you, in case you would not challenge me anon for forgetting the matter which I had in hand . . . (*View*, p. 16)

It is obvious that Eudoxus is consistently the more moderate one, appealing to given and general principles of law, ethics and politics to counter Irenius's advocacy of extreme measures, based on his bitter experience. When, for example, he claims the necessity of

> new framing as it were in the forge all that is worn out of fashion; for all other means will be but lost labour by patching up one hole to make many . . . (*View*, p. 93)

Eudoxus roundly rejects such wholesale "innovation" as foolish:

> . . . and not as ye suppose to begin all as it were anew and to alter the whole form of the government, which how dangerous a thing it is to attempt, you yourself must needs confess . . . For all innovation is perilous . . . it may hazard the loss of the whole. (*View*, p. 94).

IV

Finally, what insights into Spenser's thought about Ireland are afforded by the combined study of his images of Irish incivility and of the *View* as dialogue? Primarily, perhaps, the use of these two approaches can make us freshly aware of the complex ironies and contradictions which, as I have noticed at the outset, characterize that thought and the circumstances out of which it arises. The two different focuses throw light on two of the main aspects of the English problem with Ireland as it presented itself in the late sixteenth century.

First, the major and obvious tension in the historical situation out of which the *View* came was between Irish actuality, in all its factional complexity and instability, and the English concept of order which was being applied to it. (This is so if for the moment we take the Old English as ultimately part of the general awkward problem of the Irish, a position to which they certainly seem consigned by Spenser's furious assertions of their degeneracy.[42]) But both in the *View* and in *The Faerie Queene* V, a second struggle on a smaller scale, arising out of and contained within the first, also plays an extremely important role: that between the New English administrations based in Ireland and the central government authority in England about policies and practice in Ireland.[43] When one takes both these facets of the situation into account, it is clear that the immoderate anger of Irenius has a complex of causes: if one focuses on the major historical issue, between English as a whole and Irish as a whole, then one will notice primarily the railing against Irish incivility and turpitude; if on the other hand one concentrates on the difficult relations between the centre and outpost, it is the gap between English strategy for the government of Ireland, and the formation and implementation by local officials of detailed tactics based upon it, which appears as the main occasion of Irenius's frustration.

Solon his Follie (Oxford, 1594), the Irish dialogue of Richard Beacon,

Spenser's fellow official and undertaker in the Munster plantation, affords a suggestive analogue to the attitude of Irenius.[44] More elaborately literary and erudite than Spenser's, Beacon's work is based on a *prosopopeia*, borrowing its two central speakers, Solon and Epimenides, from Greek history, and aligning England with Athens and Ireland with Salamina, the Athenians' persistent and troublesome enemy. Solon, as narrated in Plutarch, assumed his famous madness as a licence to urge the necessity of making vigorous war on Salamina at a time when this policy was officially discredited. The parallel with Solon is invoked by Beacon to allow him preach the urgency of effective suppression of Irish dissent and rebellion and fairly frankly to criticize what he presents as the inadequacies and halfheartedness of current policies, making the work another expression of New English and planter dissatisfaction and impatience with the handling of Ireland by higher authority. In his prefatory address to the reader, Beacon threatens to become a wild man if effective action is not soon taken in Ireland. Unless his pleas get a sympathetic hearing, he promises to forsake "the pleasaunt fieldes, and meddowes" and

> henceforth take up my habitation amidst the rocks and deserts, where my arrowes may not pearce, nor the strength of my bowe withstand the bitter windes, and the harde and hoary frostes, where I shall no more play the foole with Solon in the marketplace, but the wilde man in the desertes.[45]

In both cases, as in the satiric indignation of Colin Clout, a righteous rage is being assumed as a deliberate gesture. It is not, of course, necessary to assume that such rage is not genuinely felt, just because it can be understood as part of a literary convention (in this case that of the justified rough anger of the moralist and satirist which is the motivating force of Spenserian and much other Renaissance pastoral).[46] Aesthetic forms are not ethically and ideologically neutral, but the effective and inescapable means of articulating moral and political positions. In fact one might align this indignation and air of extremism with the first term of a major implicit contradiction in Spenser's political position: that between the desire to counsel bluntly coercive courses of action and the obligation to preserve a humane distance and be seen to uphold civility.[47] Thus the tension between the reactions of the colonist *in situ* – hatred, indignation, desire for revenge, all mingled with fear – and the aspira-

tions of the urbane humanist intellectual finds expression not merely in
the content of Spenser's writing, but also in its formal gestures.

It is even possible to read this extremism of Irenius, no doubt against
the grain of Spenser's conscious intention, as an ironic shadow version
of the native wildness imputed to the Irish themselves, his antagonists
and the very objects of his ainmus. It is, of course, true that even if he
is harsh, angry, and extreme, *his* wildness is, so to speak, textual – as I
have suggested, a conscious and staged literary pose or attitude and
therefore at first sight utterly different from that of the alien Irish, whose
condition, as we have seen, Spenser strongly feels to be irredeemable.
(Their incivility might be described as invincible, like the ignorance
attributed to heathens in traditional Catholic theology.) But it is nevertheless significant that the assumption of an explicitly pastoral guise to
express indignation both by Beacon, in his threat of ascetic withdrawal
from civil society, and by Spenser himself in *Colin Clout* and *The
Shepheardes Calender*, entails the deployment of the same motifs as the
descriptions of wild men as aliens which we have seen employed to
encompass the Irish. The satirist's roughness was normally derived in the
Renaissance (by a famous false etymology) from that of the satyrs,
woodland monsters. And further, if we apply the analogy with the
Toxaris, Irenius is quasi-barbarian, outlandish Scythian to Eudoxus's
sane, centrist Greek. As Scythians are to Greeks and wild men are to the
civil, so the Irish are to the English; but so too, in a sense, are the colonists and officials in the field to the distant metropolitan policy-makers.
And so too, in his stern reproachfulness, the reforming Protestant poet-
satirist is to the corrupt court and church.[48] Thus the biographical and
historical subject Spenser, who would be regarded as the agent of civility,
in a sense places in the position of wild men – severe critics of the court,
church and state establishment – some of the most forceful among his
personae both prose and poetic. Colin Clout brought to Ireland becomes
as a native. Hence the literal and radical alterity in the major English-
Irish encounter is rehearsed again in the Eudoxus-Irenius dialogue, in
which the tensions between the remote central government and the New
English on the ground in Ireland repeat *in parvo* those between civilized
Christian Englishmen and the quasi-barbarian Irish natives. This may
seem a perverse reading, and no doubt it does not, as I have said, conform to intentionalism; but it would be unwise to attribute simplicity or
too great a singleness of motive to Spenser. As I have sought to show,
his descriptive accounts of Ireland taken as a whole reveal a marked

uncertainty of perspective: impulses in opposite directions, rage and disgust yielding to idealization and moments of imaginative identification; and a scrutiny of the workings of the dialogue form in the *View* disposes of the too ready conclusion that Irenius wins the argument.

In the first main section of this discussion my purpose has been to show how Spenser's descriptions of the Irish, whether in his prose or his poetry, have the status of symbolic representations – mediated by preexisting conventions of interpretation and necessarily formulated out of them – rather than pure reflections of the phenomena of late sixteenth-century Ireland, drawn merely from life or fact. In the second, I have been arguing for a fuller awareness of the fictive mode of existence of the *View*, and against the treatment of it as an expository document. The two investigations, of course, overlap, and as I have said at the beginning they have in common the project of viewing Spenser's, and by implication all writing, as simultaneously textual and political, fictive and discursive, and of refusing any disjunction between the realms of symbolic representation and social practice. Rhetoric and symbol are not overlays or adornments to mask the real matter and what is fictive is not thereby trivial. But these two perspectives also combine to reveal, I believe with especial and renewed clarity, the subtlety and complexity of Spenser's, and perhaps also his contemporaries', thought about, and difficulties with, Ireland.

For their encouragement and assistance in the conception and writing of this essay I am grateful to Anne Fogarty, Tom Dunne, Dorinda Outram and especially Trevor Joyce.

1. See Canny, "Edmund Spenser and the Development of Anglo-Irish Identity", *Yearbook of English Studies* 13 (1983), 1-19; Brady, "Spenser's Irish Crisis: Humanism and Experience in the 1590s", *Past and Present* 111 (1986), 17-49; Norbrook, *Poetry and Politics in Renaissance England* (London, 1984); Greenblatt, *Renaissance Self-Fashioning* (Chicago, 1980).

2. Martines, *Power and Imagination: City-States in Renaissance Italy* (London, 1979), p. 266.

3. Greenblatt, p. 192, and see Norbrook, Ch. 5. The force of such arguments has not been recognized in all quarters: see Sheila T. Cavanagh, " 'Such was Irena's Countenance': Ireland in Spenser's Prose and Poetry", *Texas Studies in Language and Literature* 28 (1986), 24-50.

4. (Utrecht, 1986). Leerssen's work might be more searching theoretically, but is a very full and informative account of writings on the Irish and Irishness, noticing, among other groups of writings, those of Spenser's close English predecessors and successors. For a discussion of the fate of these representations in the succeeding century, see my " 'Cheap and Common Animals': The English Anatomy of Ireland in the Seventeenth

Century", in T. Healy and J. Sawday (ed.) *"Now Warre Is All The World About"*: *English Literature and the English Civil Wars* (Cambridge, forthcoming). See also J. O. Bartley, *Teague, Shenkin and Sawney* (Cork, 1954).

5. Quinn, *The Elizabethans and the Irish* (Ithaca, 1954); Muldoon, "The Indian as Irishman", *Essex Institute Historical Collections* 3 (1975), 267-89; Hulme, *Colonial Encounters: Europe and the Native Caribbean* (London, 1986); Pagden, *The Fall of Natural Man: The American Indian and the Origins of Comparative Ethnology* (Cambridge, 1982).

6. See the discussion below of *The Faerie Queene* VI.iv.4ff.

7. "The Forms of Wildness: Archaeology of An Idea", *Tropics of Discourse* (London, 1978), p. 166.

8. White, pp., 165-6.

9. White, p. 172; Bernheimer, *Wild Men in the Middle Ages* (Cambridge, Mass., 1952), pp. 113ff.

10. "The Ideology of Colonization in England and America", *William and Mary Quarterly* 30 (1973), 573-598. See also Pagden on Spanish colonial ideology.

11. Canny (1973), 580.

12. See Steven Ellis, *Tudor Ireland* (London, 1985), p. 223, and Canny (1973), 583; see also Alan Ford, *The Protestant Reformation in Ireland* (Frankfurt, 1981).

13. On transhumance, see Jean M. Graham, "Rural Society in Connacht 1600-1640" in N. Stephens and R. Glasscock (ed.), *Irish Geographical Studies* (Belfast, 1970), pp. 192-207. I am grateful to Kevin Whelan for this reference.

14. See, for example, *View* 159, 160. It has been pointed out to me by Robin Hughes that this language strongly recalls that of contemporary anti-vagrancy statutes. See 39 & 40 Eliz. Cap. III, IV; 7 & 8 Jac. I Cap. I, G. W. Prothero (ed.), *Select Statutes* (Oxford, 1965); see Hughes's University of York M.A. thesis (1983) on criminal stereotypes in sixteenth-century English popular literature.

15. See the "Brigants" in *The Faerie Queene* VI.x who show the mark of villainy, the failure to plough and sow, as do the evil cannibals in VI.viii who kidnap and start to sacrifice Serena. Both groups live in remote habitations unfit for humankind, as do the "villeins" in II.ix who erupt out of woods and caves and fall at dusk upon the House of Alma.

16. See the graphic contemporary accounts of the resultant delaying of the 1584 Commission to survey the escheated Desmond property in Munster after the rebellion (*The Munster Plantation* (Oxford, 1986), pp. 8-10, 13).

17. See for example I.vii.29, V.v.11, V.viii.29, 37-8, and VI.ii.39; and see Michael Leslie, *Spenser's "Fierce Warres and Faithfull Loves": Martial and Chivalric Symbolism in The Faerie Queene* (Cambridge and Totowa, N.J., 1983), pp. 55, 72-3.

18. Brady, 48.

19. In his edition of *The Faerie Queene* (London, 1977), note on VII.vi.35 (paraphrasing Angus Fletcher).

20. Ormond, the queen's cousin and much favoured at court, who was so much a thorn in the side of the New English and particularly of advocates of coercion such as Spenser's admired Lord Grey, is a good example of such figures. See Ellis, pp. 280, 283-5.

21. *Colin Clout* 1. 183; *View*, p. 49.

22. For this account of dialogue, I have drawn upon the following discussions: Elizabeth

Merrill, *The Dialogue in English Literature* (New York, 1911), C. J. R. Armstrong, "The Dialectical Road to Truth: The Dialogue" in P. Sharratt (ed.), *French Renaissance Studies 1540-1570* (Edinburgh, 1976), Roger Deakins, "The Tudor Prose Dialogue: Genre and Anti-Genre", *Studies in English Literature* 20 (1980), 5-25, and Katherine Wilson, *Incomplete Fictions: The Formation of English Renaissance Dialogue* (Washington, D.C., 1985).

23. For a detailed account of the pervasiveness of set dialogue and disputation in sixteenth- and seventeenth-century education, see Patricia Coughlan, *Classical Themes and Influences in the Poetry of Andrew Marvell*, unpublished Ph.D. thesis, London University, 1980, Ch. 1.

24. Werner Jaeger, quoted in *Oxford Classical Dictionary* (Oxford, 1970), article on "Dialogue, Greek", p. 337; see Voegelin, *Plato* (Baton Rouge, Louisiana, 1966), p. 11.

25. Deakins, 23. Rudolf Agricola's much reprinted *De Inventione Dialectica*, completed *circa* 1479, was the classic earlier Renaissance treatise on the subject.

26. Armstrong, pp. 42-3.

27. Greenblatt, p. 164.

28. Martines, p. 271. Marx called Spenser "Elizabeth's arse-kissing poet" (quoted in Norbrook, p. 311, n. 80).

29. See M. Bakhtin, *The Dialogical Imagination: Four Essays*, tr. C. Emerson and M. Holquist (Austin, Texas, 1981).

30. Bakhtin, pp. 184, 220.

31. *The Works of Edmund Spenser: A Variorum Edition*, ed. E. Greenlaw, C. M. Osgood and F. M. Padelford (Baltimore, 1938-), Vol. X, Appendix I, p. 460; for the forfeit, see Harvey, *Marginalia*, ed. G. C. Moore Smith (Stratford-on-Avon, 1913), p. 53.

32. On the untypicality of the *Toxaris* among Lucian's works, see C. P. Jones, *Culture and Society in Lucian* (Cambridge, Mass., 1986), p. 57.

33. Erasmus sent his version to the Bishop of Winchester, writing: "I hope that it may not be altogether unacceptable to your Excellency: for it preaches friendship, an institution so holy that it was formerly held in reverence even by the most savage tribes"; and he goes on to notice the difference Lucian makes between the two interlocutors' manner of speech, characterizing that of Toxaris as "wholly Scythian in atmosphere, direct, unsophisticated, rough, earnest, serious, and manly" (Letter of 1 January 1506, *Correspondence of Erasmus*, tr. R. A. B. Mynors and D. F. S. Thomson (Toronto, 1975), Vol. II, pp. 101-3).

34. See also Lucian's other dialogue called *The Scythian*, in which an earlier Scythian namesake of this Toxaris becomes assimilated to Athenian life and is found "dressed in the Greek fashion, without sword or belt", wearing "no beard", and speaking Greek like "An Athenian born, so completely had time transformed him" – a suggestive reversal of the degeneration of the Old English in Ireland in Spenser's eyes.

35. As Ciarán Brady does at one point (p. 41) in his discussion of the *View* – though perhaps as a rhetorical ploy, which is abandoned later.

36. "'Some Quirk, Some Subtle Evasion': Legal Subversion in Spenser's *A View of the Present State of Ireland*", *Spenser Studies* 6 (1986), p. 163, n. 13.

37. V. N. Volosinov, "Reported Speech" in L. Matejka and K. Pomorska, ed. *Readings in Russian Poetics* (Ann Arbor, Michigan, 1978), pp. 149ff.

38. A topic illuminatingly discussed by Baker.

39. *View*, pp. 39-40. See Martines, p. 268, on the scorn of high humanists such as Picco-
    lomini for such material.
40. Sigonio, who is repeatedly mentioned by Spenser's Cambridge mentor Gabriel
    Harvey, says the main speaker should not only represent the opinions of the author
    clearly and unambiguously, but must win the argument (Deakins, p. 13) – not perhaps
    a programme carried out with conspicuous success by the *View*.
41. Deakins, pp. 9-10.
42. As Steven Ellis remarks, however English the Old English Catholics might still have
    considered themselves, in fact by the late Tudor period "after the breach with Rome
    . . . and the growing consciousness of differentiation from continental Europe which
    accompanied the Elizabethan idea of an 'elect nation', a narrower definition of
    'Englishness' emerged, from which the Catholic Old English were clearly excluded"
    (p. 319).
43. Spenser's defence of Grey is of course a part of this struggle, which gave rise to the
    frustration of such officials – Sir John Davies is another example – with central
    administrations which they perceived as negligent and uncooperative. For a very
    illuminating longer view of the increasing divergence of interest between Anglo-Irish
    colonists and the mainland leading, paradoxically, in the end to eighteenth-century
    colonial nationalism, see Nicholas Canny, "Identity Formation in Ireland: The
    Emergency of the Anglo-Irish" in Canny and A. Pagden (ed.), *Colonial Identity in
    the Atlantic World, 1500-1800* (Princeton, New Jersey, 1987).
44. On Beacon, see Alexander Judson, "Spenser and the Munster Officials", *Studies in
    Philology* 44 (1947), 157-73; on his role as a Munster planter, see McCarthy-Morrogh.
45. *Solon his Follie*, "The Author to the Reader".
46. Several good examples are afforded by Spenser's *Shepheardes Calender*, in the
    Renaissance tradition of Christian pastoral of which the Neo-Latin eclogues of
    Mantuan are the model. See Leonard S. Grant, *Neo-Latin Literature and the Pastoral*
    (Chapel Hill, North Carolina, 1965); Patrick Cullen, *Spenser, Marvell and
    Renaissance Pastoral* (Cambridge, Mass., 1970); and Anthea Hume, *Edmund Spenser:
    Protestant Poet* (Cambridge, 1984).
47. This contradiction is well analysed by Ciarán Brady. See also Canny (1983).
48. On the cast of Spenser's Protestantism, and his reforming or prophetic pastoral, see
    Hume and Norbrook.

The Colonization of Language: Narrative Strategy in A View of the Present State of Ireland and The Faerie Queene, Book VI

ANNE FOGARTY

I

Edmund Spenser raises many thorny questions for historians and literary critics alike. Perhaps the most urgent of these concerns the impossibility of relating what seem to us very disparate aspects of Spenser's career. On the one hand, one encounters Spenser the statesman actively involved with the forces of coercive violence in his society, while on the other, one engages with the poet of high civilization whose declared intention in writing *The Faerie Queene* was "to fashion a gentleman or noble person in vertuous and gentle discipline".[1] How, one wonders, to put this clash of perceptions in an even more extreme light, can Yeats's poet of the delighted senses be one and the same with the writer whom Karl Marx dismissed in no uncertain terms as a sycophantic supporter of Elizabethan imperialism?[2]

As a means of reconciling these radical contradictions, many scholars have practised a highly selective vision in accommodating their experience of reading Spenser's work to their concept of what the role and function of the Elizabethan writer should be. Often, Spenser's political views are simply discounted or else discarded. In particular, they are seen as an embarrassment or an impediment for the reader of *The Faerie Queene*. Not infrequently Spenser's work is protected by a grim determination to keep the role of poet and of Elizabethan colonist permanently distinct. C. S. Lewis, however, registers in his writings the difficulties of preserving such a distinction. In his analysis of Book V of *The Faerie Queene*, he maintains that the violent excesses of Artegall and of the "iron man", Talus, are an indication of the gradual corruption of Spenser's imagination and a direct by-product of his allegiance to a "detestable policy in Ireland".[3] Yet, while Lewis recognizes the intersection of Spenser's political and poetic affiliations, he uses this insight as evidence of an impermissible contamination. Where the poet's ideologies obtrude and break the surface of his work, there his poetry falters. The only recourse for the reader is to reject such writing out of hand. In the final reckoning, Lewis is persuaded that our natural moral outrage will allow us to perform a silent censorship of the poem.[4] Through such excisions the merely ideological is easily jettisoned, while the illusion is preserved intact that true poetry exists in an apolitical sphere of its own. However, elsewhere, Lewis acknowledges the complications of Spenser's position and makes the tantalizing claim that *The Faerie Queene* is the "work of one who is turning into an Irishman".[5] Here, it is clear that Lewis, despite his earlier qualms, sees that Spenser was not only tainted but also indelibly marked by the colonial experience in Ireland. In this revised reading, the traces of history cannot so easily be eradicated from Spenser's work. Rather, they are evident in everything the poet produced.

Pauline Henley in a pioneering study of the influence of Ireland on Spenser grapples with similar problems.[6] Like Lewis, she recognizes the tensions and oppositions in Spenser's life and thought. However, she deals with these tensions by seeing them in terms of frozen polarities within the poet's character. Thus, she refers to the "two warring personalities in Spenser", pointing out that his writings represent the perpetual divide between the uncompromising intransigence of the politician and the labile sensitivities of the poet.[7] Moreover, Henley discredits Spenser's political views by arguing that they are derivative and eminently forgettable, especially when compared with the originality of his poetic achievement.[8] Ultimately, she feels that we must turn a blind eye to Spenser's pronouncements as a statesman and government official because then his ideas were "moulded by his time" and thus remain lodged in the time warp of history.[9] His poetry, in contrast, preserves in her view a much more authentic voice and is, as a result, capable of transcending the bounds of history. Once again, *The Faerie Queene* has been salvaged for a modern audience, but only by dint of ripping it from its context and severing its connections with that political extremism which is such a marked aspect of the Spenserian legacy.

This false separation of aesthetics and politics does much, however, to mask vital interconnections in the *oeuvre* of this Elizabethan functionary. It is not sufficient to declare Spenser a politician in the one instance and a poet in the other, as the mood moves us. Moreover, the tacit division of labour between historians and literary critics in the field of Spenser studies has done its share in producing partial and often lopsided readings of his work.[10] The initial premise of this article is that *A View of the Present State of Ireland* and *The Faerie Queene* should be seen in a continuum, as mutually defining intertexts, rather than as conflicting expressions of a divided mentality.[11] Furthermore, it will be contended that both these texts are vitally concerned with constructing and working out the internal contradictions of a discourse of colonialism. While it is recognized that the term colonialism can merely serve as an approximate and unsatisfactory description of the complexities of English policy in sixteenth-century Ireland, it will nonetheless be argued that the images of Otherness at the core of each of these works, an untamed Ireland in the *View* and the idealized but imperilled pastoral world of Book VI, are indicative of the writer's attempt to formulate and construe a rhetoric of colonial power.[12] Furthermore, it is evident that all of Spenser's work evinces a passionate concern with the mediatory function of language and with the shaping and thereby political force of rhetoric. For him writing is, in Foucault's phrase, "the prose of the world".[13] It is the medium through which the social world is explored and contained. The interpretative function of words and the uncovering of that "secondary discourse of commentary", which Foucault sees as the fundamental aim of all Renaissance cultural production, are the central means employed by Spenser to project his programme of colonial reform in the *View* and to present the political mythologies of *The Faerie Queene*.[14] In short, for Spenser, as for any other Elizabethan writer, there is no easy line of demarcation between the rhetoric of politics and the rhetoric of fiction.[15] The two interweave and entwine in a seamless web of language or, to use a more Spenserian metaphor, they intersect in an endless labyrinth of words.

The differences between Spenser's prose treatise and his epic poem are perhaps so glaring and obvious that the similarities are often ignored.

Both are, in fact, rhetorical constructs which look at history through the optics of narrative. Both, too, problematize the dual processes of narration and interpretation in an effort to circumvent and defuse tensions created by otherwise intractable realities. Using these points of connection as a basis, the central project of this essay will be to examine the narrative strategies of the *View* and of Book VI of *The Faerie Queene* in order to pinpoint the extent to which Spenser's deployment of language and of rhetoric is inextricably bound up with his political worldview. In particular, it will be argued that language in these texts both resolves and perpetuates fracture. Although malleable to particular ends, its copiousness threatens to undermine any structure which it upholds. Thus, anxiety in Spenser is generated not alone by his ambition to construct a rhetoric of colonialism, but also by his desire to control the substance of all discourse and to attempt the colonization of language itself.

II

It has long been recognized that the *View* is the product of that crisis of mind which beset so many Elizabethan state officials in sixteenth-century Ireland.[16] Suspended between two cultures and political regimes, a striking number felt impelled to explore and justify their position in writing.[17] As Nicholas Canny has pointed out, this new echelon of colonists, the so-called "New English", was caught in a complex crossfire of interests between the hatred of the native Irish, the disgruntled opposition of the Old English, the exigencies of their official duties, and the call of their own private ambition.[18] Thus, a significant feature of Elizabethan colonial literature is that it is written on the defensive and designed not alone to express the prerogatives of the Crown, but also to protect and promote the interests of the individual author.[19] In this light, the language of officialdom espoused by Spenser acquires a new aspect. It may now be seen to be at the service of dual and at times opposing interests. The antiquarian, governmental, military, legal, and bureaucratic codes which predominate in the text have the ostensible purpose of establishing a cohesive policy of control and reform in Ireland, but they simultaneously fulfil a secondary goal by providing leeway for the formulation of a self-identity which would otherwise remain unexpressed. Spenser in the *View* speaks as a subject in both senses of the term. He is at one and the same time setting forth proof of his loyalty and assiduity as the subject of Elizabeth I and shaping and giving contour to his own subjectivity. The *View* may hence be counted as a prime example of the Renaissance activity of self-fashioning, identified by Stephen Greenblatt, whereby rhetoric becomes the arena in which the contesting claims of authority and of the subject are enacted.[20] By inserting himself within the interstices of official thought, Spenser acquired the freedom to give vent to his own frustrations and feelings, and to voice his own desires. The zealous reformulation of colonial structures in Ireland is, then, as much an expression of thwarted ambition as of a committed belief in authoritarian order.

This uneasy marriage of purposes helps to explain, in part, those divisions and contradictions which have caught the attention of almost every commentator on the *View* since its first publication. James Ware, for example, in the preface to the first edition of the text in 1633, observes that "although it sufficiently testifieth . . . learning and deepe judgement, yet we may wish that in some passages it hat bin tempered with much more moderation".[21] Here, Ware notes the disjunctive nature of the *View* and attributes this impression to the stark contrast between the writer's circumspect erudition and the stridency of his political opinion. Indeed, in terms of its narrative dynamics, Spenser's text seems to be torn between two countervailing movements. On the one hand, it pretends to order and control by rewriting the chaos of Irish history in the ratiocinative prose of the logician and bureaucrat, while on the other it dallies and delays, splintering into numerous side-tracking commentaries and observations which threaten to undermine the symmetrical patterns previously laid down. An undertow of narrative excess constantly engulfs the measured advance of ideas. As a result, many of the altercations between Eudoxus and Irenius revolve around the problems of narrative control. Irenius sets up an overarching structure at the beginning of the dialogue:

> I will then according to your avisement begin to declare the evils which seem to be most hurtful to the common weale of that land, and first those which I said were most ancient and long grown; and they also of three kinds: the first in the laws, the second in customs, and last in religion.   (*View*, p. 3)

This framework, however, breaks down under the impact of his straying arguments. He frequently scolds Eudoxus for causing him to digress:

> I was about to have told you my reason therein, but that you
> yourself drew me away with your questions,   (*View*, p. 10)

or pointedly curtails his own comments in order to keep matters within bounds. Thus, he cuts short his comparison of the Scythians and the Irish:

> Many such customs I could recount unto you, as of their old manner
> of marrying, of burying, of dancing, of singing, of feasting, of curs-
> ing, though Christians have wiped out the most part of them by
> resemblance whereof it might plainly appear to you that the nations
> are the same, but that by the reckoning of these few which I have
> told unto you, I find my speech drawn out to a greater length than
> I purposed.   (*View*, p. 59)

Likewise, he decides to limit his account of the corruption of the clergy in Ireland:

> I could perhaps reckon more, but I perceive my speech to grow too
> long, and these may suffice to judge of the general disorders which
> reign amongst them.   (*View*, p. 89)

Eudoxus, for his part, also takes Irenius to task for blatantly departing from the matter in hand. He expresses amazement at Irenius's cross-comparisons of Ireland and Scotland:

> I wonder, Irenius, whither you run so far astray, for whilst we talk
> of Ireland, me thinks you rip up the original of Scotland; but what
> is that to this?   (*View*, p. 38)

In a similar vein, he is driven to caustic comment, following Irenius's own voluntary disruption of his reflections on the degeneracy of the Old English:

> In truth, Irenius, ye do well to remember the plot of your first pur-
> pose, but yet from that meseems ye have much swerved in all this
> long discourse of the first inhabiting of Ireland, for what is that to
> your purpose?   (*View*, p. 48)

At times, Eudoxus goes so far as to cast aspersions on Irenius's attempts to persuade him of the pertinence of his rambling arguments. The irony of the following retort is, for instance, patent:

> Ye bring yourself, Irenius, very well into the way again, notwithstanding that it seemeth that ye were never out of the way.
>
> (*View*, p. 49)

On other occasions, Eudoxus loses the thread entirely and must be brought to tether by Irenius when his objections become too unsettling. Thus, Eudoxus points out that Irenius's plans for creating a lasting peace in Ireland are paradoxically obsessed with making provision for a never-ending state of war in the country:

> But as for these garrisons which ye have now so strongly planted throughout all Ireland and every place swarming with soldiers; shall there be no end to them? For now thus being, meseemeth, I do see rather a country of war than of peace and quiet which ye erst pretended to work in Ireland. (*View*, p. 140)

Irenius's reply in this instance is significant. In order to prevent further misunderstanding, he assures Eudoxus that he will "in private, discover the drift of (his) purpose" (*View*, p. 140). Hence, he intimates that his previous narration was a type of drifting which cloaked rather than revealed his intentions. These latter have instead to be unearthed, with great care, in another place. There is also a suggestion that the drift of narrative is deliberately protective of his designs and that the hither and thither of his sinuous discourse is an elaborate play or feint which is needed in order to cover up the internal contradictions in his political designs for Ireland.[22] The hidden effects of ideological strain are thus articulated by the disputes between Eudoxus and Irenius concerning the ordering and import of the discourse of colonialism which they are setting in motion. The difficulties with narrative transitions can be seen to mark moments of slippage within their construct of ideas. However, at the same time, the pointed welding together of the dialogue becomes a prominent advertisement for the triumph of rhetoric over circumstance. Irenius and Eudoxus never fail to congratulate themselves on their ability, albeit at times a very parlous one, to control their medium. They incessantly exchange compliments during the course of their talk as if thereby to assure us of the validity and efficacy of their discussion. Here, a few examples must suffice. Eudoxus, for instance, praises Irenius for his defence of Lord Grey:

> Truly, I am very glad to hear your judgement of the government of that honurable man so soundly,   (*View*, p. 20)

and admires Irenius's skill in arriving at conclusions about cultural history on the basis of scanty evidence:

> Your conceit is very good and well fitting for things so far from certainty of knowledge and learning only upon likelihoods and conjecture.   (*View*, pp. 61-62)

Similarly, Irenius extols Eudoxus's disquisition on the benefits of improving landlords:

> Ye have well, Eudoxus, accounted the commodities of this one good ordinance,   (*View*, p. 83)

and gratefully acknowledges his timely reminder about the ultimate aim of their debate:

> I see, Eudoxus, that you well remember our first purpose and do rightly continue the course thereof.   (*View*, p. 141)

Thus, by a skilful inversion, the barely negotiated narrative shifts and transitions are an essential strategy for indemnifying the political ideology relayed in the *View*. Through holding the threat of imminent narrative collapse at bay, Irenius and Eudoxus succeed in consolidating their political beliefs. The mastery of narrative form becomes on one level an objective correlative for that total imposition of control central to the reforms which they propose. The colonization of language acts as an instructive lesson in the methods to be adopted by colonialism in the political sphere. The final irony, of course, is that this establishment of order in the *View* is precarious and the result of vigilant scrutiny and review. Only by constantly checking themselves can Irenius and Eudoxus ensure some measure of jurisdiction over the boundaries of their talk. In the long run, however, their efforts are doomed to failure and a sub-text of disorder and chaos continues permanently to baulk the fixity of Irenius's "perfect plot".

In a recent explication of *The Shepheardes Calender*, Jonathan Goldberg puts forward the argument that Spenser's first major literary work is marked by a dispersal of voices and names.[23] He points out that the poem is made up of an interweave of multiple well-nigh nameless voices, ranging from the pronouncements of the elusive Immerito and his allegorical counterpart Colin Clout, to the shadowy but pervasive comments of the editor, E.K. In a similar fashion, diffusion of voice is a central motor force in the *View*. The counterpoint created by the converging and diverging thoughts of Eudoxus and Irenius is but one aspect of this process. Far more remarkable is the manner in which their speeches are scored by the confluence of numerous interpretative codes. The vocabularies of juridical, military, anthropological, historical, and ethical investigation all form part of the rich repertoire of expression exploited in their discussion. To this exent, the *View* is a form of *bricolage*, that is, a discourse which is patched together by borrowings from other linguistic systems and sub-systems. In his account of the *bricoleur* at work, Derrida explains that this reliance on diverse source materials is due to the perception that any given structure of meaning is inevitably incomplete.[24] The *bricoleur* is, in short, the rag and bone man of language who gathers his bric-a-brac of words as a gesture against impending impoverishment. Thus, the proliferation of codes in Spenser may be attributed to the failure of language to encapsulate total meaning, while at the same time it can be recognized as a defensive strategy designed to by-pass this inadequacy.[25] Irenius and Eudoxus, as a result, constantly introject other voices and attempt, in Sidney's phrase, to tell those things which cannot be shown.[26] Of such "intermeddlings" the most striking are the absorption of the voice of language and that of authority. Both of these, it is implied, speak themselves and insinuate their way with ease into the flow of the text.

One cannot fail to notice that Eudoxus and Irenius lavish considerable time and energy on the definition of individual words. Eudoxus frequently demands clarification of items of vocabulary, especially those which seem unusual to him. Not surprisingly, the words which cause him most pause are those which describe facets of Irish life and customs; they reify that quality of strangeness which he associates with the "salvage nation". In this manner, for example, he questions the term "Brehon Law":

> What is that which you call Brehon Law? It is a word to us
> altogether unknown,   (*View*, p. 4)

and also the concept of "coign and livery":

> I do not well know, but by guess what ye do mean by these terms of
> coignye and livery, therefore I pray you explain them.   (*View*, p. 34)

Sometimes, he requires an explanation to be delivered *post hoc*, even
when he is reasonably sure that he has understood the word in context.
It is as if definition of this kind is necessary in order to stabilize and
delimit meanings which would otherwise remain in flux. Such is his
motivation, for instance, in requesting added information about the Irish
custom of "kincogish":

> This custom of Kincogish, the which word I would be glad to know
> what it namely signifieth, for the meaning thereof, I seem to under-
> stand reasonably well.   (*View*, p. 36)

The etymology of a word is for Eudoxus the final frontier. Once this has
been drawn up, meaning and signification, or in current terminology
signifier and signified, assume a clear and unequivocal identity, and the
threat of uncertainty is removed. Few words, indeed, resist the efforts of
Eudoxus and Irenius to wrestle them into patterns of meaning consonant
with their political ends. Etymology becomes, then, one of their
foremost weapons for marshalling and controlling the ambiguities of
language. By laying bare the origins of words, they uncover a nexus of
meaning which seems to be preordained by a linguistic system greater
than themselves. Only the slightest encouragement is needed on their part
to lure these hidden connections out into the open.

A closer look at an isolated example of such philological privateering
will clarify their methods of operation. Eudoxus, playing his usual role
of straight man, asks Irenius to provide a definition of the term "county
palatine". Irenius, as a matter of course, applies the tools of linguistic
analysis in his reply:

> It was I suppose first named Palatine, of a Pale as it were a pale and
> defence to the inner lands, so as now it is called the English Pale;
> and thereof also is a Palsgrave named, that is an Earl Palatine,

others think of the Latin *palare*, that is to forage or outrun, because
those marchers and borderers use commonly to do so; so as to have
a County Palatine is in effect but to have a privilege to spoil the
enemy's borders adjoining; and so surely it is used at this day as a
privileged place of spoils and stealths, for the county of Tipperary,
which is now the only County Palatine in Ireland, is by abuse of
some bad ones made a receptacle to rob of the counties about it.

(*View*, p. 30).

The aptly chosen etymologies appear to feed effortlessly into the
political commentary which ensues. The first and more definitive source
of origin to Irenius's way of thinking, that of "pale" or "defence",
serves to elucidate the correct function of a county palatine, whereas the
more dubious affinity of the concept with the Latin "palare" is mentioned in order to explain the Irish corruption of a prior established
meaning. In this way, the ability of language to reflect on its own content
becomes part of a further circular pattern by virtue of which the history
of words is forcibly interlinked with Irenius's unfolding account of
atrocity and disorder in Ireland. Through its very reflexivity, language is
made appear transparent and in association the marked prejudice of the
comments of Eudoxus and Irenius can assume a type of functional
innocence. Political commentary is circuited through the internal workings of language and is delivered whole and entire, almost it would seem
without the aid of human intervention.[27] Thus, the frequent etymologiz-
ing in the *View* is far more than scholarly affectation. Rather, it becomes
a potent tool in the development of a colonial rhetoric which succeeds
expertly in advancing its arguments while always carefully concealing
their mode of construction. This process is rendered all the more complex because the narrative foregrounds the explanations of words with
such assurance. The apparent consistency of linguistic analysis blinds us
with its logic and clarity, while all the time deflecting our attention from
the insidious rationale which underpins it. Language itself appears to col-
laborate in a political conspiracy and to duplicate endlessly the
experience of colonial history in its own internal structure.

This intermeshing of linguistic and political practices may be compared to a similar dovetailing of the motions of private desire and the will
of authority. Irenius and Eudoxus emphasize their collusion with a
source of power beyond themselves and brandish the fact that all of their
pronouncements are integral parts of a secondary discourse of inter-

pretation. Their interchanges claim to do no more than reveal provisions
and frameworks which already exist. At the end of the dialogue, Irenius
even disavows all originality of thought on his part by confessing that his
proposals have merely been a reprise of the ideas of others:

> Not that I take upon me to change the policy of so great a kingdom
> or prescribe rules to such wise men as have the handling thereof, but
> only to show you the evils which in my small experience I have
> observed to be the chief hindrance of the reformation thereof. And
> by way of conference to declare my simple opinion for redress
> thereof, and establishing a good course for that government; which
> I do not deliver for a perfect plot of mine own invention to be only
> followed, but as I have learned and understood the same by the con-
> sultations and actions of very wise governors and counsellors whom
> I have sometimes heard treat thereof, so have I thought good to set
> down a remembrance of them for mine own good and your satisfac-
> tion.   (*View*, pp. 169-70)

To apply the distinction of Russian Formalism, Irenius's declamations
and reconstructions represent the *sjužet* of the narrative, while the
authoritative insights of the "wise governors and counsellors" to which
he refers constitute its *fabula*.[26] However, as Peter Brooks points out, it
is the permanent dilemma of the *sjužet* that the *fabula* will always elude
its grasp.[29] It remains a mythic construct beyond the scope of any narration. Irenius describes his speech as "a remembrance" and in this light
his dialogue with Eudoxus may be viewed as an eternal retrospective on
a predetermined structure of order which it can never fully encompass.
Even the formal frame of their discussion stresses its iterative nature.
The text begins *in medias res*. The opening statement delivered by
Eudoxus points backwards to previous comments made by Irenius about
Ireland:

> But if that country of Ireland whence you lately came be so goodly
> and commodious a soil as you report . . .   (*View*, p. 1)

The discourse about to commence is thereby divested of its uniqueness
and situated within a chain of similar encounters between these two
interlocutors. A comparable feeling of infinite regress is elicited by the
ending of the dialogue when Irenius and Eudoxus promise to circle back

on terrain already covered, in order to make good deferrals and omissions necessitated by the rigour of the talk which they have just concluded:

> I thank you, Irenius, for this your gentle pains withal, not forgetting now in the shutting up to put you in mind of that which you have formerly half promised that hereafter, when we shall meet again upon the like good occasion, ye will declare unto us these your observations which ye have gathered of the antiquities of Ireland.
>
> (*View*, p. 170).

It is noteworthy that at both of these junctures Ireland becomes emblematic of a pleasure which is both frustrating and endlessly enticing. At the beginning, the focus shifts from Irenius's delight in Ireland as a "goodly and commodious . . . soil" to his elaboration of the vexations of the country. The conclusion, in contrast, suggests a motion in the opposite direction; the memory of "evils" and "hindrances" cedes to the pleasurable anticipation of a conversation about various details of Irish antiquity. Thus, the *View* circles back perpetually on itself. The economy of individual desire, as represented by Irenius and Eudoxus, ceaselessly reproduces the hidden mandates of the *fabula* of order and relentlessly constructs in the course of this operation the intricate tangle of colonial rhetoric.

The principal ideology invoked in the *View* to give expression to the claims of authority is that of the body politic. Elizabethan iconography is permeated by a belief in the inviolable identity of the monarch and her state. Many portraits of the queen represent this interconnection in cartographic terms. The oft-cited Ditchley portrait, for example, depicts Elizabeth as standing on a map of England, with her richly textured gown obliterating the features of the globe beneath her.[30] The entire political order is subsumed in the iconic figure of the queen, while the map which acts as a synecdoche for her subject people effectively cancels their presence from the scene. On a general level, it can be argued that representations of this kind served to mystify the nature of power, and to substitute the aura of symbolic concord for the reality of social conflict. Spenser in the *View* resorts to similar totalising metaphors in order to project the mythic goal of social harmony which lies at the heart of the colonial dream. In particular, the text emphatically upholds the indivisibility of the queen's Irish dominions and the reach of her authority. Irenius triumphantly declares that "all the whole land is the Queen's" and, indeed, the entire momentum of his schemes for reform results from his belief that this formula for absolute power should be granted full credence. His ultimate aim is to leave the impress of royal command forever inscribed in the Irish landscape. In this context, Irenius may be seen as a self-appointed cartographer who controls the unknown and the intractabale by mapping it. The dialogue, accordingly, embodies his blueprint for an idealized Ireland which, through carefully executed alterations, has been transformed into a perfect icon of imperial power. Svetlana Alpers in a study of the symbolism of cartography in sixteenth- and seventeenth-century paintings points out that maps during this period constituted a new form of possessive knowledge.[31] Above all, they were accorded prestige because their very existence provided visual proof that the object represented could be commandeered and captured in its entirety. Due to the ease with which it allowed one "to see something that was otherwise invisible", mapping became a new means of objectifying knowledge and of gaining control over the world.[32] The welter of geographical and topographical information which accompanies Irenius's plans for the disposition of troops in Ireland and for the relocation and dispersal of warring Gaelic tribes "in sundry places" has the function, then, of repressing disorder by revealing invisible structures of fealty in the country. Thus, for example, his account of the province of Connaught:

> The province of Connaught containeth in the whole (as appeareth in the record at Dublin) seven thousand and two hundred ploughlands of the former measure and is of late divided into six shires or counties, the County of Clare, the County of Leitrim, the County of Roscommon, the County of Galway, the County of Mayo and the County of Sligo: of the which all the County of Sligo, all the County of Mayo, the most part of the County of Roscommon, the most part of the Leitrim, a great part of the County of Galway, and some of the County of Clare, is like to excheat unto Her Majesty, for the rebellion of their present possessors, the which two counties Sligo and Mayo are supposed to contain almost three thousand ploughlands, the rate whereof ratably to the former, I value almost at 6,000 per annum.   (*View*, pp. 129-30)

In this passage, opposition – "the rebellion of (the) present possessors" – becomes transmuted into harmony in the impassive ciphers of the military cartographer. The spoils of war metamorphose into pacific ploughlands. Hence, the punctilious listing of the individual counties of all the provinces of Ireland, and the equally precise computation of the amount and value of state holdings throughout the length and breadth of the country are not to be regarded merely as a decorative litany in the *View*. By producing compendious registers of all of the topographical, social, and political features of Ireland, Irenius is enabled to recodify the "licentious barbarism" which he so much abhors in the language of "civil conversation", and to realign the wild terrain which contains so many lurking atrocities for him. He literally writes the map of Ireland anew.

Seen in this light, his name, too, acquires added symbolic weight. If, as Gottfried proposes, one of its possible derivations is "Irena", the term used for Ireland in *The Faerie Queene*, then Irenius may be regarded as the voice of the conquered land itself, which raises a plea for its own subjugation.[33] Hence, his account of Irish affairs masks a further erasure on which the political vision of the *View* is grounded. By arrogating to himself the opinions of an entire people, Irenius inverts the rebelliousness symbolized by Ireland and turns it into submission. He does this, in particular, by collapsing his vantage point as omniscient colonist with his twin role as an allegory of the country itself. It is as if he becomes the only medium through which the land can express itself. This metaphor is chiefly sustained by the self-reflexive terminology adopted by Eudoxus and Irenius throughout the dialogue. Time and again, they refer to their "plotting" of the fate of Ireland. As Morley indicates, the major connotation of this term as used by Spenser is that of "ground plan".[34] However, it also carries the secondary meaning of stratagem or scheme. By means of this fusion of contexts, Irenius locates his plan or political grand design within the contours of the Irish landscape itself. Thus, Eudoxus, for example, describes a new topic to be broached by Irenius in terms of an expansive piece of territory in which they can roam:

Let us now pass unto your second part, which was, as I remember, of the abuses of customs, in which me seems ye have a fair champion laid open unto you, in which ye may at large stretch out your discourse into many sweet remembrances of antiquities. (*View*, p. 37)

He uses similar phrases to express his appreciation of Irenius's plans for a military campaign in Ireland: "Ye have very well meseems, Irenius,

plotted a course for the achieving of these wars,'' (*View*, p. 120) and to
praise his scheme for the plantation of Ulster: "Thus I see the whole purpose of your plot for Ulster." (*View*, p. 129)

The major effect of the "perfect plot" of the *View* is to achieve that
separation of rhetoric and violence, which Stephen Greenblatt identifies
as the ultimate aim of Spenser's bipartite schema of figures in Book V
of *The Faerie Queene*.[35] The sympathies of Eudoxus and Irenius centre
entirely on the "goodly country" of Ireland. Eudoxus, for example,
having heard an account of the early vicissitudes of Irish history, is
driven to exclaim "I do much pity that sweet land" (*View*, p. 19). What
is overlooked, however, in the onrush of this affective rhetoric is the
bloodshed which must happen in order for the colonial plot to succeed.
Irenius contrives even to present his proposals for a brutal offensive
against the dissident Irish in nullifying terms. By subtle ellipsis he makes
it appear as if this will simply be a self-administering process of
attrition:

> Although there should none of them fall by the sword, nor be slain
> by the soldier, yet thus being kept from manurance, and their cattle
> from running abroad by this hard restraint, they would quickly con-
> sume themselves and devour one another.   (*View*, p. 104)

Through this evocation of an innate cannibalism in the savage
inhabitants of the country, he effectively obscures the real causes of their
extremity. Thus, his infamous description of the Irish in the wake of the
Desmond rebellion as "anatomies of death" and "ghosts crying out of
their graves" follows an inevitable course which erases every trace of
humanity from the field of vision until all that remains is his lamentation
that "a most populous and plentiful country" has been left void and
empty (*View*, p. 104). The negative presence of the Gaelic tribes becomes
transformed into an absence and what is left behind is the free space
within which the plot of colonialism can unfold itself. Once again, a
supreme integration of ends has been achieved, whereby Spenser's out-
line of his political vision is symbolic of the methods to be used in order
for this vision to become reality. In this sense, the *View* is illustrative of
the ideology which it advocates. Narrative and political strategy coincide,
and the colonization of Ireland is made coterminous with a supporting
colonization of language.

III

Foucault's concept of the heterotopia may be used in order to set up an initial comparison between the different narrative worlds of *The Faerie Queene* and the *View*. In a posthumously published article, he propounds the theory that societies maintain themselves by incorporating within their structures "other spaces", or oppositional sites, in which the many facets of their ideologies and belief systems may be simultaneously represented, contested and inverted.[36] While these counter-sites may involve an idealizing moment, Foucault ultimately distinguishes them from the non-place of utopia and prefers instead to refer to them as heterotopias, that is places of Otherness or difference. Moreover, despite being "absolutely different from all the sites that they reflect and speak about", heterotopias remain inseparably linked with reality.[37] As a result, Foucault positions them both inside and outside of social reality. He cites as examples such varied socio-cultural structures as ships, brothels, boarding schools, military academies, gardens, cemeteries, honeymoon trips, and cinemas. In addition, he suggests that two distinct kinds of heterotopia may be discerned: those which create real spaces imbued with order in the attempt to offset the jumbled and disordered nature of social reality, and those which create an illusory or fictional space so as to criticize and expose certain aspects of social and political regimes. There is, however, a glaring omission from this account of the role of other spaces within culture, namely literature and writing. It will be argued here that both the *View* and Book VI of *The Faerie Queene* conform to Foucault's description of the heterotopia. Within the other space afforded by writing, both of these texts are concerned with constructing a revised version of social and political order, while still acknowledging their connections with the material and historical circumstances in which they are embedded. Thus, the *View* formulates its vision of control and reform within terms of the difficulties experienced by colonists in sixteenth-century Ireland, while the pastoral and mythic world of Book VI presents itself as a reflection of and a commentary upon the actualities of the Elizabethan court.

Furthermore, these two texts provide examples of the two different categories of heterotopia described by Foucault. The *View* may be seen as a heterotopia of compensation because the regulated world which it envisions seeks to replace the difference and instability represented by Irish barbarism with the uniformity of English rule. As is customary in such colonial fictions, the image of the savage native functions as a type of Doppelgänger for the civilized conqueror, delimiting an area of prohibition and projecting his fears of what he may become.[38] Ultimately, the irrational Otherness associated with Ireland becomes the major impetus for the vision of political order and control put forward by the *View*. Book VI of *The Faerie Queene*, on the other hand, constitutes an illusory heterotopia because it sets in motion fictions through which the contradictions of the contemporary political scene may be laid bare and analysed. Unlike the *View* which aims at reducing everything to a levelling sameness, it openly invites the play of difference as a means of countermanding chaotic relations in the world beyond it. In the final event, however, the narrative of the poem is almost destroyed by the images of difference which it unleashes and the only recourse left to the poet is to undermine and censor his own creations in an attempt to stem the dangerous energies to which they expose him.

First, it is important to note the extent to which metaphors of colonialism are imbricated with Spenser's description of the imaginative process in *The Faerie Queene*. These images come particularly to the forefront in the proems to the successive books of the poem. In Book II, for example, it is claimed that "the happy land of Faery" is not just a "painted forgery", but is as real as the new worlds which have been placed on the map through the Elizabethan voyages of discovery:

> But let that man with better sence advize,
> That of the world least part to us is red:
> And dayly how through hardy enterprize
> Many great Regions are discovered,
> Which to late age were never mentioned.
> Who ever heard of th'Indian Peru?
> Or who in venturous vessel measured
> The Amazons huge river now found trew?
> Of fruitfullest Virginia who did ever vew? (II. Proem. 2)

The narrator, here, validates the truth of his creation by destabilizing the relationship between reality and fiction. In fact, he goes so far as to assert that the method by which new countries are annexed in reality parallels the process by which the meaning of the poem unfolds. Thus, political rhetoric and the language of fiction are seen in terms of each other. Both ultimately depend on the colonization of language and on the knowledge and mastery of words. It is implied too that if the book may be seen as world, then the world may also be seen as book. This is particularly stressed by the pun on the word "to read" at the begining of the stanza:

> But let that man with better sence advize,
> That of the world least part to us is red.

"Red", in this context, means both to reveal or disclose, and to read or interpret. Hence, for Spenser, we construe or read the world in the same way that we make sense of poetry. As a result, the interpretative skills of the reader are taxed in *The Faerie Queene* with particular intent. By problematizing our ability to decipher and understand, the text aims at educating and controlling our political responses. Also, it will be seen that, in tandem with this process, the poem constantly subverts and questions its own rhetoric as a means both of revealing and of protecting the ideology it enshrines.

The primary problem with which we are confronted at the opening of Book VI is that of the seductiveness and endlessness of fiction itself. Text and reality can no longer be held apart and the narrator depicts himself as aimlessly wandering in a world of language. Words have become inexhaustible and beyond any form of control:

> The waies, through which my weary steps I guyde,
> In this delightfull land of Faery,
> Are so exceeding spacious and wyde,
> And sprinckled with such sweet variety,
> Of all that pleasant is to eare or eye,
> That I nigh ravisht with rare thoughts delight,
> My tedious travell doe forget thereby;
> And when I gin to feele decay of might,
> It strength to me supplies, and chears my dulled spright.
> (VI. Proem. 1)

This sense of impediment extends also to the subject matter of the book which is about to commence. The virtue of courtesie is missing in the real world of the court and subsumed entirely as fictive ideality in the figure of the queen herself. Elizabeth, as transcendent signifier, nullifies the narrator's efforts in advance. His words falter in their attempt to capture her presence, as the clumsy periphrases illustrate:

> . . . where may be seene
> The goodly praise of Princely curtesie,
> As in your selfe, O soveraine Lady Queene,
> In whose pure minde, as in a mirrour sheene,
> It showes, and with her brightnesse doth inflame
> The eyes of all, which thereon fixed beene;
> But meriteth indeede an higher name:
> Yet so from low to high uplifted is your name. (VI. Proem. 6)

The echoing phrases of the final two lines bear witness to the difficulty
of the poet's position. His aim is to exalt the transcendent authority of
the queen – to lift her name from low to high – but yet, at the same time,
he must recognize that his undertaking is doomed to failure before he
even begins. The "higher name" which he seeks will never be located and
the words which he uses will always, as a consequence, be haunted by an
absence or lack. In the end, the poem resigns itself to being an elaborate
circumscription of the fictions of authority. Its circulation of meanings
will reproduce in another guise the mechanisms by which power sustains
its mystique in society:

> Then pardon me, most dreaded Soveraine,
> That from your selfe I doe this vertue bring,
> And to your selfe doe it returne againe:
> So from the Ocean all rivers spring,
> And tribute backe repay as to their King. (VI. Proem. 7)

It is noteworthy that Spenser derived this cameo narrative of fealty
from the colonized topography of Ireland, as the tidal currents of the
Shannon are given particular mention elsewhere in the poem.[39] Thus, the
formalized obeisance of *The Faerie Queene* and of his defence of colonial rule in the *View* stems from a similar belief in the unassailable
prerogatives of royal control.

Moreover, by including his work within the never-ending cycle of an
ocean which feeds rivers which feed an ocean, the poet succeeds in
enmeshing his private desire with the designs of power. It will be a signal
feature of this desire that it sustains itself by trying to satisfy the lack
which it wishes to fill, while at the same time always leaving it gaping.
In this connection, two key images of the proem must be borne in mind.
the motifs of a vision which is adumbrated but never fully revealed in
stanza 6, and of the spiralling circularity of royal power in stanza 7:

Right so from you all goodly vertues well
Into the rest, which round about you ring, (VI. Proem. 7)

will be reflected and repeated in varying forms during the course of Book
VI. Through such self-replicating structures, the narrative propels itself
onwards while always acknowledging its ultimate status as the echo
chamber of a power which remains obdurately remote and intangible.
Thus, the irony of the central plot of the *Legend of Courtesie* is that it
must constantly stress Elizabeth's presence as an absent cause and
celebrate her as an outside authority which both upholds and permanently undermines its fictions.

From the outset, the quest of Calidore, the exemplary hero of Book
VI, is linked with the problems of language and of narration. Indeed, it
is underlined that this figure's plight is but a transposition of the narrator's dilemma. Both are afflicted by the endless nature of their undertaking. Thus, Calidore's first account of the enterprise which faces him
immediately recalls the words of the proem:

> . . . now I begin
> To tread an endlesse trace, withouten guyde,
> Or good direction, how to enter in,
> Or how to issue forth in waies untryde,
> In perils strange, in labours long and wide. (VI.i.6)

The task which he has been set is, of course, to hunt down and kill the
Blatant Beast. This hybrid monster is never described directly, but seems
to be a curious anthropomorphic mixture of dog, hydra, and wild boar.
From the end of Book V onwards, it runs amok through the poem
inflicting poisonous, festering wounds on several of the characters.
Critics have generally seen in the Beast a figure of slander or detraction,
one derivation of its name being from the Latin "blatire", to babble or
to bark.[40] The text, however, also intimates that the Blatant Beast represents all the abuses of rhetoric, in short, the disruptive and falsifying
powers of language itself. Thus, the "thousand tongs" of the Beast are
described in Canto xii:

> And therein were a thousand tongs empight,
> Of sundry kindes, and sundry quality,
> Some were of dogs, that barked day and night,

> And some of cats, that wrawling still did cry,
> And some of Beares, that groynd continually,
> And some of Tygres, that did seeme to gren,
> And snar at all, that ever passed by;
> But most of them were tongues of mortall men,
> Which spake reprochfully, not caring where nor when. (VI.xii.27)

Hence, Calidore seeks to subdue and tame the anarchic forces of language, a mission which will inevitably remain unaccomplished. It is no surprise, then, that his attempts to close quarters with the proliferating babble of languages symbolised by the Beast seem so ineffectual and irrelevant.[41] Indeed, there are many indications that this monster represents a repressed libidinal aspect of the mannered world of courtesie, and that it is a splinter function of the seductive, chivalric heroes who abound in Book VI. Calidore's courtesie, for example, displays itself primarily through his ability to converse and to use words in order to manipulate situations.[42] Far more given to discourse than to action, he persuades Briana and Crudor to renew friendly relations, seals the peace between Priscilla and her father by treating him to a carefully edited version of her exploits, engages in dialogue with Meliboee concerning the relative merits of urban and rural lifestyles, and seeks to dispel Colin Clout's anger by luring him into a discussion of the blissful scene on Mount Acidale, which he had so fatefully interrupted. As a final flourish of irony, Pastorella in the gloom of the Brigants' cave recognizes this most talkative of heroes by his voice.

A complex network of connections, in fact, links the Beast with the suppressed instinctual world which is the dark underside of courtesie. Its first appearance in the book coincides with Calidore's interruption of the love-play of Calepine and Serena. Far from being discomfited by this blunder, he displaces their previous activity with the "delightfull pleasure" of conversation, thereby setting the scene for the eventual wounding of Serena by the Blatant Beast. Thus, Calidore substitutes the sublimations of language for the instinctual pleasures of physical satisfaction. He uses words as a means of rerouting and containing the motions of desire. However, the wound inflicted by the Beast marks the repressions or lack in such discourse. A similar juxtaposition occurs during Calidore's conversation with Colin Clout. While listening to the latter's explanations, he exhibits that greed for words which is one of his principal characteristics:

In such discourses they together spent
Long time, as fit occasion forth them led;
With which the Knight him selfe did much content,
And with delight his greedy fancy fed,
Both of his words, which he with reason red;
And also of the place, whose pleasures rare
With such regard his sences ravished,
That thence, he had no will away to fare,
But wisht, that with that shepheard he mote dwelling share. (VI.x.30)

However, the next stanza cancels this moment of transport and reminds us of the wound of desire which impels Calidore's actions:

But that envenimd sting, the which of yore,
His poysnous point deepe fixed in his hart
Had left, now gan afresh to rancle sore,
And to renue the rigour of his smart. (VI.x.31)

Once again, the deflectionary pleasures of rhetoric are interrupted by the libidinal forces which they are designed to hold in check. The power of words to seduce is shown to be complementary to the Beast's power to erode and dissipate meaning. Calidore, who is associated with the voicing and expressiveness of words, is inevitably accompanied by the Blatant monster who allegorizes that desire which both motivates and impedes the use of language. Thus, these two figures represent interlinked rather than opposing forces and, as a result, neither can ever succeed in definitively routing the other.

On another level again, the disruptive sorties of the Beast are emblematic of the meanderings and fracture of Spenser's narrative as a whole. The randomness of the monster's attacks and the devious trails which it lays for its pursuers mirror the constant ruptures in the plot of Book VI. All of the main protagonists, in contrast, show a deep-seated predilection for the symmetrical, harmonious endings of romance. Calidore unites Briana and Crudor, pairs off Tristram and the lady of the nameless, discourteous knight, salvages Priscilla's reputation, restores Pastorella to her parents, and is even granted a momentary Pyrrhic victory over the Blatant Beast itself. Calepine, who acts as a surrogate for Calidore, is no less industrious in the production of happy endings. He passes on the baby whom he has rescued to the childless

Matilde, and saves Serena in the nick of time from the depredations of
the cannibal race. Arthur, likewise, metes out punishment to the discourteous Sir Turpine, thus putting an end to his crimes, and rescues
Timias, his squire, from the grips of Disdaine and Scorne. However, run-
ning counter to all these attempts to achieve conclusive and idyllic
endings, is a far more powerful momentum which destroys any
equilibrium which has been attained. As Harry Berger indicates, almost
every episode after the first canto is left unresolved.[43] Stories are interrupted and then discontinued, despite the narrator's protestations that he
will supply us with further information at a later point. Thus, the futures
of Tristram, the noble Savage, Matilde's child, and of Priscilla and
Aladine remain a blank. Calepine and Serena are abandoned at the
moment of reunion and even the fate of Calidore and Pastorella is
hedged with uncertainty. Mirabella, too, notwithstanding Arthur's exer-
tions on her behalf, is left caught in the freeze frame of allegory, condemned continually to perform a penance which can never be completed:

> Here in this bottle (says the sory Mayd)
> I put the teares of my contrition,
> Till to the brim I have it full defrayd:
> And in this bag which I behinde me don,
> I put repentaunce for things past and gon.
> Yet is the bottle leake and the bag so torne,
> That all which I put in, fals out anon;
> And is behinde me trodden downe of Scorne,
> Who mocketh all my paine, and laughs the more I mourn. (VI.viii.24)

The suspensions created by the Ariostan endings, which occur seven
times in various guises during the course of the book, also disturb the
smooth progression of events. Each transition represents a lacuna, rather
than a moment of completion; the narrator either cuts across his own
recital and defers an ending until another occasion:

> Such chaunces oft exceed all humaine thought:
> That in another Canto shall to end be brought, (VI.iii.51),

or reminds us that events which we have just witnessed were, in fact, a
deviation from the central concerns of the plot and hence of minor
importance:

But Calidore himselfe would not retaine
Nor land nor for hyre of his good deede . . .
There he remaind with them right well agreed,
Till of his wounds he wexd hole and strong,
And then to his first quest he passed forth along. (VI.i.47)

The Beast may, therefore, be seen as a symbol of that element of imbalance in Spenser's text which constantly defies and prevents closure. Its very name lends support to this argument. The *OED* states that one of the possible roots of "blatant" is an earlier form of the word "to bleat". In this light, the Blatant Beast is a monstrous anti-type of the pastoral, arcadian world which constitutes the core of Book VI. It signals in advance that even the rounded harmony of this idyllic scene will also be overthrown and dispelled by the turbulence of Spenserian narrative.[44]

Indeed, this pastoral episode is one of the major cruxes in the *Legend of Courtesie*. It has been declared a glaring desertion of duty on Calidore's part and seen as conclusive evidence that he willfully plays truant from the quest which he has been assigned.[45] However, one of the prime objectives of this departure into rural idyll is that it allows the poet to establish a heterotopic sphere from which the problems of the court may be reviewed. Just as Ireland in the *View* functions as the place of difference in which the lineaments of order may be traced, so too Calidore's sojourn amongst the shepherds serves to consolidate and redefine the virtue of courtesie. Frank Kermode makes the point that "the first condition of Pastoral is that it is an urban product".[46] Thus, the pastoral interlude permits a meeting of contraries and aims at counterposing and ultimately reconciling the conflicting values of court and country. The further purpose which this episode serves is to continue a sequence of images set in motion in the proem. A recurring *leitmotif* in Book VI is a scene of scopic desire which centres on the iconic figure of a woman whose presence can only be partially captured and represented.[47] In the wake of the impeded vision of the queen in the proem, the text attempts by various subterfuges to produce a succession of metonymies for this vital, but perpetually blurred, originary point. This method of duplicating similar images by infinitely embedding them in each other may be likened to the heraldic device of the *mise en abîme* where a miniature version of the overall design is inset at the centre of a shield.[46] Through this process of interior duplication, Spenser's text repeats and reworks a central scene in an effort to combat the tensions with which it is laden.

The first and most disturbing of these scenes is that of Serena amongst the cannibals. It acts as a nightmare inversion of the visionary idealism which marks the opening of this book. Serena is described in terms of the voyeuristic lust of the cannibals, who feast their eyes as a prelude to the utimate consumption which they eagerly await:

> So round about her they them selves did place
> Upon the grasse, and diversely dispose,
> As each thought best to spend the lingring space.
> Some with their eyes the daintest morsels chose;
> Some praise her paps, some praise her lips and nose;
> Some whet their knives, and strip their elbows bare:
> The Priest him selfe a garland doth compose
> Of finest flowres, and with full busie care
> His bloudy vessels wash, and holy fire prepare. (VI.viii.39)

She is dissected and violated by the invasive seeing of this "salvage nation" and of the narrator who shares their point of view. The scene culminates with a triumphant blazon which tries to provide an exhaustive inventory of her beauty:

> Her yvorie necke, her alabaster brest,
> Her paps, which like white silken pillowes were,
> For love in soft delight thereon to rest;
> Her tender sides, her bellie white and clere,
> Which like an Altar did it selfe uprere,
> To offer sacrifice divine thereon;
> Her goodly thighes, whose glorie did appeare
> Like a triumphall Arch, and thereupon
> The spoils of Princes hang'd, which were in battel won. (VI.viii.42).

However, as Barthes has argued, such enumerative descriptions always fall short of their objects.[49] The more Serena is exposed to the rapacious eyes of those surrounding her, the more she is anatomized, and the more she disappears from sight. In the course of this fragmentation, she is reduced, in Barthes's phrase, to a kind of "dictionary of fetish objects".[50] Ultimately, Spenser lets loose the ravening gaze of desire in order to curb it and place it under restraint. Thus, even barbarism in the poem is discovered to have its limits. In the final reckoning, it is answerable to the dictates of a rudimentary "civilitie". As a result, two moments of censorship cut short this episode. First, the cannibals check their own impulses and are prevented by their priest from defiling Serena because, as the text informs us, "religion held even theeves in measure" (VI.viii.43). Then, the entire scene is curtailed by the providential arrival of Calepine. In the closing moments of the canto, the two principal figures are left sitting in the dark. Serena's nakedness becomes its own disguise; she is denuded, but shrouded in darkness. She both can and cannot be seen. The poet, like the cannibals, refuses any further intrusions. The scene is truncated and Serena is thereby effectively removed from our field of vision, never to be seen again, despite the narrator's promise to the contrary:

> So all that night to him unknowen she past.
> But day, that doth discover bad and good,
> Ensewing, made her knowen to him at last:
> The end whereof Ile keepe untill another cast. (VI.viii.51)

In the final two visionary scenes of Book VI, both of which occur during Calidore's stay in the world of arcadian innocence, the symbolic female figures assume a more idealized shape, and appear increasingly nebulous and elusive. Pastorella, for example, is depicted simply as a stock pastoral character, namely, the youthful maiden, who is the epitome of uncorrupted beauty:

> And soothly sure she was full fayre of face,
> And perfectly well shapt in every lim,
> Which she did more augment with modest grace,
> And comely carriage of her count'nance trim,
> That all the rest like lesser lamps did dim:
> Who her admiring as some heavenly wight,
> Did for their soveraine goddesse her esteeme,
> And carolling her name both day and night,
> The fayrest Pastorella her by name did hight. (VI.ix.9)

Her very name obscures; it depends on an omission and on those elliptical strategies which Richard Cody identifies as a fundamental aspect of pastoral fiction.[51] We learn only that she is a beautiful shepherdess and the perfect accoutrement of the fictional world in which she resides. Later, she loses even this identity when Calidore returns her to her parents, Claribell and Bellamour. She becomes ultimately an incarnate but cryptic sign. The purple rose birthmark on her breast allows her genuine origin to be ascertained. But, in the final event, she remains anonymous, as her real name is never revealed in the poem. Pastorella metamorphoses before our eyes, and in the end, like Serena, she foils the attempts of language to fix or establish her presence in any definitive way.

In the final, climactic vision on Mount Acidale, a tension is set up between Calidore's wish to understand and interpret, and his longing for passive voyeuristic pleasure:

> He durst not enter into th'open greene,
> For dread of them unwares to be descryde,
> For breaking of their daunce, if he were seene;
> But in the covert of the wood did byde,
> Beholding all, yet of them unespyde.
> There he did see, that pleased much his sight,
> An hundred naked maidens lilly white,
> All raunged in a ring, and dauncing in delight. (VI.x.11)

However, in this case, the perspectives provided by the text are even more blurred and confused than in the previous scenes of scopic desire. Only with difficulty does the eye focus on the fourth Grace who is the central aspect of this phantasmic scene. It does not zoom in on her as in the description of Serena. Instead, this new icon of beauty remains indistinct and framed by her Otherness:

> And in the middest of those same three, was placed
> Another Damzell, as a precious gemme,
> Amidst a ring most richly well enchaced,
> That with her goodly presence all the rest much graced. (VI.x.12)

The qualifying comparison which is unfolded in the following stanza deliberately deflects our attention from this "damzell" whose presence has been so fleetingly evoked. We are forced to look in another direction:

Looke how the Crowne, which Ariadne wore . . .
Being now placed in the firmament,
Through the bright heaven doth her beams display,
And is unto the starres an ornament,
Which round about her move in order excellent. (VI.x.13)

A final attempt at description also runs aground. The poet, recognizing
the futility of his task, foreshortens his account of events, and simply
repeats his earlier comments in slightly altered form:

Such was the beauty of this goodly band,
Whose sundry parts were here too long to tell:
But she that in the midst of them did stand,
Seem'd all the rest in beauty to excell,
Crownd with a rosie girlond, that right well
Did her beseeme . . . (VI.x.14)

Ultimately, the entire spectacle is dislodged and fragmented into further "sundry parts" by the explanatory interjections of the narrator, and
the long disquisition held by Calidore and Colin Clout concerning the
meaning of the episode. The anatomizing scrutiny of allegorical interpretation has replaced the fetishizing gaze of the cannibals' greed. The
language of exegesis succeeds in dismantling the arcane scene on Mount
Acidale. In this way, it protects it from further profanation, while still
subjecting it to the scopic regime of reading. It is as if the poem can continue only through the secession of its own rhetorical constructs. Thus,
the discontinuities, rather than the unity, of the vision are foregrounded.
In particular, we are reminded that the ethereal "fourth Mayd" is but
a further figure in the chain of metonymies which represents the queen
with ever-increasing obliquity:

Sunne of the world, great glory of the sky,
That all the earth doest lighten with thy rayes,
Great Gloriana, greatest Maiesty,
Pardon thy shepheard, mongst so many layes,
As he hath sung of thee in all his dayes,
To make one minime of thy poore handmayd,
And underneath thy feete to place her prayse,

>   That when thy glory shall be farre displayd
>   To future age of her this mention may be made. (VI.x.28)

Elizabeth is, once again, appealed to as the absence upon which the text
is predicated. While she is responsible for the fissures in the poem's surface, it is through probing such insufficiencies and through highlighting
the struggle of language both to express and to contain desire that *The
Faerie Queene* performs its complex act of homage to the incontrovertible
right of authority.

Spenser has been called the poet of "second thoughts" and, indeed,
the recursive patterns of his writings and their self-conscious efforts to
mould and manipulate language are the primary strategies which he uses
to articulate his political convictions.[52] As analysis of the *View* and of
Book VI has shown, both of these works present equivocal and divided
accounts of the political ideologies which they wish to sustain. In both
cases, the "other space" projected by the text – the reordered Ireland of
the *View* and the consolatory but doomed world of pastoral and faery
in *The Faerie Queene* – is realized with great difficulty. The anxieties and
contradictions which are at the core of all of Spenser's writings give rise,
in the case of the *View*, to a narrative which threatens to be engulfed by
its own copiousness, and in the case of *The Faerie Queene*, to a narrative
which flirts with and is threatened by its own ultimate breakdown. In
addition, the meandering and dilatory character of both of these works
results from a deep-rooted conflict between the stimulus of language and
the necessity to keep this incitement in check. Each of these texts polices,
interrogates and probes its own rhetoric in an attempt to protect and control the fictions of authority which they manage to construct. Anxieties
about political order are contained by being deflected onto the realm of
language, but rise persistently to the surface in the many instances cited,
both in the *View* and in Book VI, of lines of narrative which are stifled,
cut off and abandoned. Due to this continual struggle between the attrac-
tions and the prohibitions of narrative and language, Spenser's texts are,
in the final reckoning, founded on their own impossibility. The Blatant
Beast, that haunting spectre of unaccommodated Otherness, will always
remain at large in the world and the ultimate goal, that of the colonization of language, will never be attained.

1. "A Letter of the Authors . . . to Sir Walter Raleigh" in Smith and de Selincourt, p. 407.
2. W. B. Yeats, "Edmund Spenser" in *Essays and Introductions* (London, 1961), pp. 356-83. Yeats, in fact, tries to recuperate Spenser for a modern readership by presenting him as an unacknowledged rebel and a prototype of the sensual Romantic poet before the event. It is of note, however, that Yeats's essay served as a preface to his carefully streamlined edition of Spenser's work: "I have put into this book only those passages from Spenser that I want to remember and carry about with me" (p. 381); Karl Marx, "Sir Henry Summer Maine: Lectures on the Early History of Institutions" in *Die Ethnologischen Exzerpthefte* (Frankfurt, 1976), pp. 423-500. Marx's vehement denunciation of Spenser as "Elizabeth's arse-kissing poet" (p. 450) occurs during his discussion of the way in which Brehon Law was eroded in Ireland by the astigmatic policies of English colonialism.
3. C. S. Lewis, *The Allegory of Love* (Oxford, 1936), p. 349.
4. Lewis: "The rest of the book needs little comment. It is not, and ought not to be a favourite" (p. 349).
5. C. S. Lewis, "Edmund Spenser 1552-99" in *Studies in Medieval and Renaissance Literature* (Cambridge, 1966), p. 126.
6. Pauline Henley, *Spenser in Ireland* (Cork, 1928).
7. Henley, p. 144.
8. Henley: "Spenser's claim to fame owes nothing to his political opinions . . . few know more than the name of his prose work. Had Spenser been less than a great poet, it might never have seen the light" (p. 9).
9. Henley, p. 168.
10. A succession of recent publications has, however, reassessed and repoliticized Spenser's work, including Jonathan Goldberg, *Endlesse Worke: Spenser and the Structures of Discourse* (Baltimore, 1981), Stephen Greenblatt, *Renaissance Self-fashioning: From More to Shakespeare* (Chicago, 1980), and David Norbrook, *Poetry and Politics in the English Renaissance* (London, 1984).
11. The shortened title, *View*, will be used hereafter to refer to this work.
12. Ciarán Brady and Raymond Gillespie (ed.), *Natives and Newcomers: The Making of Irish Colonial Society 1534-1641* (Dublin, 1986), Nicholas Canny, *The Elizabethan Conquest of Ireland: A Pattern Established 1565-1567* (Sussex, 1976), and Stephen Ellis, *Tudor Ireland: Crown, Community and the Conflict of Cultures 1470-1603* (London, 1985) all provide stimulating, revisionist accounts of English colonial policy in sixteenth-century Ireland.
13. Michel Foucault, *The Order of Things* (New York, 1970), pp. 17-44.
14. Foucault, p. 40.
15. For example, Thomas Wilson in *The Arte of Rhetorique* (ed. Thomas J. Derrick, New York, 1982), comments on the ability of rhetoric to negotiate political advantage and declares that the pleasures of language can even outdo in impact the effect achieved by the use of violence: "For if the worthiness of eloquence may move us, what worthier thing can there be, then with a word to winne cities and whole countries? If profite may perswade, what greater gayne can we have, then without bloudshed to achieve a conquest?" (p. 6).
16. Renwick, *View*: deems that this treatise "was written in a time of unusual anxiety, and might be regarded as a contribution to government in a time of crisis" (p. 182).

17. A representative cross-section of such works may be found in James P. Myers (ed.), *Elizabethan Ireland: A Selection of Writings by Elizabethan Writers on Ireland* (Hamden, Conn., 1983).

18. Nicholas Canny, "Edmund Spenser and the Development of an Anglo-Irish Identity", *Yearbook of English Studies* 13 (1983), 1-19; the Old English were those settlers in Ireland who had, in the course of time, adapted to Gaelic ways and customs and in many cases intermarried with the native Irish.

19. Canny writes: "The point being made was that . . . the Old English lords . . . were being goaded into rebellion by the harsh, ill-advised and frequently illegal actions of English officials and soldiers whose only concern was self-advancement. This argument and the investigations that produced evidence to substantiate it, were pursued with such persistence that the New English were thrown back on the defensive and literature such as we have been considering (including the works of Spenser and Sir John Davies) was produced in defence of their actions and ambitions" (p. 13).

20. Greenblatt (1980), pp. 1-9.

21. Ware's preface is reprinted in E. Greenlaw, C. G. Osgood and F. M. Padelford (ed.), *The Works of Edmund Spenser: A Variorum Edition: The Prose Works*, Vol. 9 (Baltimore, 1949). Hereafter referred to as *Prose*.

22. In Spenser the term "discourse", in association with its Latin root "discursus", literally means to run to and fro. "Discourse" then describes the thrust and parry of rhetoric and is the word used by Eudoxus and Irenius to refer to their conversation, and by the narrator of *The Faerie Queene* when adverting to the plot of the poem. See *The Faerie Queene* (ed.) A. C. Hamilton (London, 1977), p. 675, for a brief discussion of this phrase.

23. Jonathan Goldberg, *Voice Terminal Echo: Postmodernism and English Renaissance Texts* (London, 1986), pp. 38-67.

24. Jacques Derrida, "Structure, Sign, and Play in the Discourse of the Human Sciences" in *Writing and Difference* (Chicago, 1978), pp. 278-93.

25. Terence Cave, *The Cornucopian Text: Problems of Writing in the French Renaissance* (Oxford, 1979), describes the Erasmian concept of *copia* in terms which parallel Derrida's notion of *bricolage*. In order to brook the divide between *res* and *verba*, Renaissance rhetoric depicts language as autonomous and sees the aim of writing as the ability to reflect other texts rather than reality itself. The renaissance book is a storehouse of borrowed fragments of discourse in which "it is not reality that is imitated but other writers; not ideas, but texts" (p. 19).

26. Philip Sidney, "An Apology for Poetry" in C. Gregory Smith (ed.), *Elizabethan Critical Essays* (Oxford, 1904), Vol. 1: "Many things may be told which cannot be shewed, if they knowe the difference between reporting and representing" (p. 198). Sidney, thus, implies, that it is through its indirections and allusiveness that art achieves its effect.

27. This intervention has, of course, taken place. John W. Draper in "Spenser's Linguistics in the Present State of Ireland", *Modern Philology* 17 (1919-20), 471-86, states that the most likely origin of the term is LL. *palatinus* meaning either a "chamberlain" and "palace official" or "belonging to the palatium or palace". He also points out that the correct derivation of this word was known to sixteenth-century scholars. It can, thus, be inferred that Spenser here, as elsewhere in the *View*, was indulging in that punning word-play which is such a hallmark of humanist writing.

28. Boris Eichenbaum in his essay "The Theory of the Formal Method" in Lee T. Lemon and Marion Reis (ed.), *Russian Formalist Criticism* (Lincoln, Nebraska, 1965), pp. 99-139, summarizes Shklovsky's theories concerning these two terms, story (*fabula*) and plot (*sjužet*). He explains that the story represents the raw material which is remodelled and structured by the plot.

29. Peter Brooks, *Reading for the Plot: Design and Intention in Narrative* (Oxford, 1984): "We must, however, recognize that the apparent priority of *fabula* to *sjužet* is the nature of a mimetic illusion, in that the *fabula* – what really happened – is in fact a mental construction that the reader derives from the *sjužet*, which is all that he ever directly knows" (p. 13).

30. Reproduced by Roy Strong, *Portraits of Queen Elizabeth I* (Oxford, 1963), Plate XV.

31. Svetlana Alpers, *The Art of Describing: Dutch Art in the Seventeenth Century* (Chicago, 1983), pp. 119-68.

32. Alpers, p. 133.

33. *Prose*, p. 278.

34. *Prise*, p. 278. Morley explains that the word "plotte" is used "not in a bad sense from the French *complot*, but from the English plot or plat as in grass-plots or political platforms". Elsewhere in Spenser, however, the term also has the meaning of scheme or intrigue. See, for example, *The Faerie Queene* (V.ix.47):

> He brought forth that old hag of hellish hew,
> The cursed Ate, brought her face to face,
> Who privie was, and partie in the case:
> She, glad of spoyle and ruinous decay,
> Did her appeach, and to her more disgrace,
> The plot of all her practise did display,
> And all her traynes, and all her treasons forth did lay.

35. Stephen Greenblatt, "Murdering Peasants: Status, Genre and the Representation of Rebellion", *Representations* 1 (1983), 1-30.

36. Michel Foucault, "Of Other Spaces", *Diacritics* 16 (1987), 22-27.

37. Foucault, p. 24.

38. Hence, the bulk of the wrath of Irenius and Eudoxus falls on the heads of those English settlers who had adapted to Irish ways. Eudoxus, for example, delivers a diatribe against such traitors to the cause (*View*, p. 151). See also Homi K. Bhabha, "Difference, Discrimination and the Discourse of Colonialism" in Francis Barker, Peter Hulme, Margaret Iverson, Diana Loxley (ed.), *The Politics of Theory* (Colchester, 1983), pp. 194-211, for an account of the way in which colonial texts both welcome and try to dislodge the stereotypes which are their symbolic core. Speaking of the aggression directed against black culture, he argues that "colonial fantasy . . . in staging the ambivalence of desire, articulates the demand for the negro which the negro disrupts" (p. 20).

39. *The Faerie Queene*, IV.iii.27.

40. Arnold Williams, *Flower on a Lowly Stalk* (Michigan, 1967), declares that "the Blattant Beast is merely the essential evil of slander, indeed of all discourtesy: it hurts someone" (p. 68).

41. J. C. Maxwell, "The Truancy of Calidore" in William Mueller and Don Cameron Allen (ed.), *That Soveraine Light: Essays in Honor of Edmund Spenser, 1552-1952* (Baltimore, 1952), pp. 63-9, notes that Calidore's fight with the Beast represents something of an anti-climax, while Humphrey Tonkin, *Spenser's Courteous Pastoral* (Oxford, 1972), contends that Calidore renders the Blatant Beast "almost irrelevant to the central concerns of the book" (p. 33).

42. See Shormishtha Panja, "A Self-Reflexive Parable of Narration: *The Faerie Queene VI*", *Journal of Narrative Technique* 15, 3 (1985), 277-88, who observes that Calidore is the most loquacious of Spenser's heroes and points out that discourse forms the main activity of Book VI.

43. Harry Berger Jnr., "A Secret Discipline: *The Faerie Queene*, Book VI" in William Nelson (ed.), *Form and Convention in the Poetry of Edmund Spenser* (New York, 1961), pp. 35-75.

44. Kenneth Grose, *Spenserian Poetics: Idolatry, Iconoclasm and Magic* (New York, 1985), p. 230, treats this role of the Beast as a type of anti-pastoral in greater detail.

45. Maxwell, p. 65-66.

46. Frank Kermode, *English Pastoral Poetry* (London, 1952), p. 14.

47. See Christian Metz, *The Imaginary Signifier: Psychoanalysis and the Cinema* (Bloomington, Indiana, 1982), pp. 58-78, for an account of the scopic drive. Metz explains that the desire to see "represents the absence of its object in the distance at which it maintains it and which is part of its very definition" (p. 59). In all of Spenser's scenes of voyeuristic viewing the object of desire is either destroyed and thus banished, or else it disappears and fades away from sight.

48. For a recent discussion of this concept of the *mise en abîme* see Stephen W. Melville, *Philosophy Beside Itself: On Deconstruction and Modernism* (Minneapolis, 1986), pp. 96-7.

49. Roland Barthes, *S/Z* (tr.) Richard Miller (New York, 1974): "As a genre, the blazon expresses the belief that a complete inventory can reproduce a total body, as if the extremity of enumeration could devise a new category, that of totality: description is then subject to a kind of enumerative erethism: it accumulates in order to totalize, multiplies fetishes, in order to obtain a total defetishised body" (p. 114). See also Goldberg (1981), p. 16, for a further discussion of this passage in Barthes.

50. Barthes, p. 114.

51. Richard Cody, *The Landscape of the Mind: Pastoralism and Platonic Theory in Tasso's Aminta and Shakespeare's Early Comedies* (Oxford, 1969). Cody argues that pastorals are concerned with hidden comparisons and allusive signs which insist on remaining indecipherable. He claims that the fascination of pastoral literature derives from "the difficulty of coming to a just appreciation of what the poet does not say" (p. 161). Pastorella, in Spenser's text, seems just such an example of the elliptical "non-articulation of experience" inherent in pastoral fiction which Cody describes.

52. William Blissett, "Florimell and Marinell", *Studies in English Literautre, 1500-1900* V (1965), 87-1904 (p. 89).

The Fate of Irena:
Spenser and Political Violence

RICHARD A. McCABE

Machiavelli is a perilous muse. His alleged inspiration of the political doctrines celebrated in Spenser's *Legend of Justice* has damaged the reputation of both poem and poet.[1] Readers of the 1940s and 1950s were disturbed by unpleasant similarities to the methods and attitudes of modern fascism. Even critics such as Graham Hough who laboured to defend Spenser from these associations, found in his apparent lack of compassion one of the inherent "corruptions of imperialism". According to Hough, only the "strains" and "degradations" of Spenser's Irish experience can account for the "harsh severity of his idea of corrective justice". Yet Hough's defence of *The Faerie Queene* is persistently undermined by memories of *A View of the Present State of Ireland* and he is finally driven to admit that the political allegory attempts the moral defence of "something indefensible".[2] Thus the shift from "fascism" to "imperialism" proves counter-productive.

Spenser could hardly be expected to have seen matters in the same light. As applied to *The Faerie Queene* Hough's concept of "imperialism" is at least as anachronistic as the popular recourse to "fascism". Although there are many points of contact between Machiavelli and Spenser, their final outlooks are radically different. In Spenser, arguments from political "necessity" go hand-in-hand with allusions to "the singular providence of God" whose wisdom "miraculously" guides the course of human destiny (*View*, p. 44). His political analysis quite consciously eschews any suggestion of amorality. Indeed it is precisely this insistence upon moral justification that has fuelled the controversy and led to Spenser's denunciation as either hypocrite or bigot. The purpose of the present essay is neither to condemn nor exonerate Spenser's political philosophy but to examine the complex process whereby the blunt recommendations of the prose were transformed into the idealised vision of the poem, the process whereby political violence became a moral imperative within a fundamentally providential world-view.

Spenser's reception of Machiavelli was qualified by personal experience of life in Tudor Ireland. Towards the end of *A View* he cites the *Discourses on Livy* to the effect that order may be achieved only through the imposition of a strong, central military authority. He commends Machiavelli for "worthelye" contrasting the attitudes of the ancient Romans with those of Renaissance Italians who

> used to limitt theire Chief officers so streightlye as that theareby some times they have lost suche happie occacions as they could never come unto againe, the like wheareof who so hathe bene Conversante in the governement of Irelande hathe to often sene to theire greate hurte. (*View*, p. 229)

Machiavelli is deemed valuable in that his observations provide an apparently objective historical perspective upon Spenser's own.[3] His call for a more "ample and absolute" power could not, therefore, be dismissed as the product of eccentricity or faction. The logic of conquest endorsed it. In Spenser's view, Tudor England owed its advanced level of civilization to the regulating presence of the monarch whereas Ireland, denied such a central authority, had declined into a state of "salvage" regression. Since it was impossible for the English sovereign to reside in the conquered territory, as Machiavelli had recommended in *The Prince*, the Lord Deputy was to receive the powers of Vice-regent.[4] As such he could respond to "the necessitye of present occacions" taking "the sodaine advantage of time which beinge once loste will not be recovered" (p. 229). "Necessitye" is obviously a key word.

Spenser speaks of the necessity for political violence in terms which recall Machiavelli's much-maligned doctrine of "reason of state". He advocates the military use of famine, the dispersal of conquered nations, and the colonization of conquered territory. Critics of Machiavelli had used similar doctrines to allege the fundamental corruption of his political thought. Innocent Gentillet's *Anti-Machiavel* (1576) had identified "ragione di stato" as the supreme index of princely corruption.[5] The villainous "Machevill" who serves as prologue to Marlowe's *Jew of Malta* is virtually a personification of Gentillet's polemic. His disciple, Barabas, is ludicrous in his self-centred isolation whereas the essence of true Machiavellian thought is statecraft. The popular "Machiavellian" exults in his evil whereas gloating exultation is as foreign to the tone of Machiavelli's canon as is complacent moralising. Spenser avoids either extreme. Perhaps his most striking debt to his mentor is the remarkable candour of his style. *A View* makes no secret of its attitudes, its use of the concept of "necessity" is both frequent and unashamed. Subtler minds than Gentillet's had examined and endorsed "reason of state". Botero, Budé, du Vair, Montaigne, and Lipsius were amongst the list of illustrious humanists who found the moral platitudes of the "ideal prince" topos wholly inadequate to the realities of political life.[6] It was not that the end justified the means but that in practice necessity was often perceived to dictate both: reason of state could be a matter of national survival. There can be little doubt that such, in the proper circumstances, was Spenser's opinion, yet "reason of state" remains insufficient to explain the tone of *A View*. If Spenser merely gestured towards traditional morality while remaining staunchly "secular" his treatise would be far less problematic than it is. Fundamental to his outlook, however, is the more venerable doctrine of the "just war", defended by theologians from Augustine to Aquinas, and beyond.

According to Augustine it is the injustice of the opposing side that imposes upon the innocent the necessity of waging just wars.[7] The terminology is familiar. Necessity is again a central issue but the emphasis has changed. Not expediency but *moral* necessity is now in question. It is a moral and spiritual imperative to wage certain wars despite the violence this entails. Augustine proceeds to say that although this is true, it is nevertheless to be regretted. Similarly in the first book of *The Faerie Queene*, Heavenly Contemplation tells St. George that the time will come to cleanse his hands "from guilt of bloudy field:/ For bloud can nought but sin, and wars but sorrowes yield" (I.10.60). However, as this "time" has not yet arrived he must return immediately to the rigours of the active life. This dual Augustinian view proved most congenial to

Spenser, supported as it was by the code of chivalry which informs the entire poem. In preaching the Second Crusade in 1147, St. Bernard of Clairvaux had insisted upon a new ideal of Christian militarism. Dedicated to the founder of the Templars, his treatise *De Laude Novae Militiae* in a sense institutionalised the concept of the "just war" in relation to the duties of knighthood.[8] Heroic tradition, already established in the *Song of Roland*, responded enthusiastically. With the menace of Islam still oppressive, Ariosto and Tasso could legitimately adapt medieval themes to Renaissance contexts. Spenser followed much the same course in effectively equating the service of Gloriana with the service of God (I.10.59), thereby dismissing Philip II as the "proud Paynim King" (I.18.8). More is involved here than courtly compliment or abuse. The Christian/Paynim dichotomy provides Spenser with a means of organising his political allegory. The "pagans" of romance fiction are the Catholics of reformed politics: Duessa is first seen accompanied by a Saracen knight (I.2.12). By implication the Reformed campaign against Catholicism takes on the moral urgency of a Renaissance Crusade, Luther and Calvin supplanting St. Bernard. Hence the moral necessity of the use of the "Sword" which Spenser defines as "the royal power of the Prince, which ought to stretch itself forth in her Chief strength to the redressing and cutting off of all those evils which I . . . blamed" (*View*, p. 97). Spenser's work marks the apotheosis of a Reformation commonplace. Hovering in the background to *The Faerie Queene*, with its predictions of a final great battle between the forces of Gloriana and those of the "Paynim" king, are the millenarian tendencies of Protestant Apocalyptic historiography.[9]

One must, therefore, be cautious in interpreting Spenser's intentions. Correspondences with Machiavelli, however illuminating in their immediate context, may finally prove misleading. By "necessity" Spenser often means moral necessity even when more practical or immediate considerations contribute to the argument. The two types of "necessity" may, of course, overlap whenever moral duty and political expediency point in the same direction. Yet many of Spenser's suggestions for the government of Ireland are by no means practical and would, as the Privy Council knew, have greatly inconvenienced the Tudor state. Spenser's moral earnestness often impairs the soundness of his political thinking; the crusader takes precedence over the civil servant. For example, whereas the government viewed Lord Grey's tenure of office as a disastrous failure, Spenser regarded their attitude as an act of moral betrayal. Throughout *A View* he uses the word "reform" with all the electrifying associations of "reformation". No less than the "perpetual reformation" of Ireland is in question (*View*, p. 109). He thus casts the battle for Ireland as one episode in the continuing war for the soul of Europe. But religious reformation must be preceded by the "sword" because of the "salvage" state of the nation concerned. Ironically Ireland's acutest political observer was also its least sympathetic; Spenser's research into the "antiquities" of the island led him to draw comparisons with distant British history (*View*, p. 143). The "present" state of Ireland was that of a living fossil and the duty of the Tudors was to force the country into a new age of Protestant enlightenment. Hence the insistence upon the civil policies of education and redevelopment which were to follow the "necessary" use of the sword. Although the argumentation is both confused and self-contradictory the Irish are "proved" to be of barbarous Scythian descent and, therefore, peculiarly in need of such education as the conqueror alone could bestow (*View*, p. 58). One has only to recall the emphasis upon physical discipline in contemporary educational tracts to appreciate the solipsistic nature of the analogy: the adult is superior to the child, as the conqueror is superior to the vanquished.

Spenser's racial vocabulary is strikingly similar to that employed in treatises describing the denizens of the New World.[10] Indeed in a letter of advice to Lord Grey, Sir Henry Sidney had compared certain Irish clans to cannibals.[11] Naturally wretched, the state of the Irish nation is exacerbated by its "Romish" religion. In terms of statecraft this was a useful political tool and could be exploited accordingly. To dismiss it as merely a politic tool, however, would be a grave mistake. Spenser means what he says and so did his patron, Lord Grey. According to Grey the Irish "addiction" to "treachery and breach of fidelity" is directly attributable to a defective religion which "dispenses" with political oaths for "advantage".[12] Proceeding further still, Spenser suggests that the Catholicism of the "mere" Irish springs less from spiritual conviction than from political defiance (*View*, p. 161). As a result, it cannot be expected to exercise any appreciable effect upon the moral character. The real danger in all this, and the one which dictated Grey's action at Smerwick, was that people so ignorantly disaffected would welcome the intervention of the Spanish and in so doing hasten the end of the Protestant English state.[13] A letter written by Lord Grey to Burghley in 1572 contains an interesting association of ideas. First of all Grey alludes to

"the late horryble and tirannical dealings in France" which have become
known to history as the St. Bartholomew's Day Massacre. He then
expresses the hope that "her majesty may have the wisdom to follow and
magnitude to execute the things that may divert the same from hence".
His third and final topic of concern is the prospect of his own appoint-
ment to Ireland. Though never asserted, the connection is clearly
implied. Mutual understanding renders explanation redundant.[14]

Grey shared Spenser's belief that the island to which he planned to
come was a place devoid of moral or political order. Although Spenser
understood the fundamental principles of the Brehon Law, he chose to
regard it merely as a codified perversion of natural justice. Artegall's
chief opponent is none other than Grandtorto (Great Tort), a corruption
so gigantic as to necessitate the immediate implementation of the
vigorously "thorough" policy for which Grey, Spenser, and Lodowick
Bryskett so persistently called. "Thorough" is the shibboleth of their
faction.[15] As Irenius explains, "wheare no other remedye maie be
devized nor no hope of recouerie had theare muste needs this violente
meanes be used". As the word "recouerie" suggests, the destructive
nature of the necessary violence is sublimated into images of physic and
husbandry:

> for all those evils must first be cut away by a strong hand before any
> good cane be planted like as the corrupt branches and unwholesome
> boughs are first to be pruned and the foul moss cleansed and scraped
> away before the tree can bring forth any good fruit. (*View*, p. 95)

But just as pruning must be undertaken at the appropriate time, so
Grey sought to take "advantage" of the critical moment in the 1580s and
Spenser believed that the opportunity then lost had at last recurred. The
"present" state of Ireland was the auspicious season. The abandonment
of the "thorough" policy by Sir John Perrot had subjected the country
to the curse of political mutability, "which too-too true that lands in-
dwellers since have found" (VII.6.55). Perrot's perception of the role of
Lord Deputy was radically different from that of Grey whose mangled
reputation Spenser continued to defend long after he could hope for any
reward in terms of patronage, indeed long after Grey's death.[16] The
defence was born of a deeply shared philosophy.

Grey's family rejoiced in a distinguished tradition of service to the
state reaching back to the reign of Henry III. In the sixteenth century

they were amongst the first of the old aristocratic families to accept the tenets of the Reformation. William Grey, father of Spenser's patron, was one of the few who rallied to Northumberland's assistance in his attempt to usurp the throne for Lady Jane Grey. David Lloyd captured the essence of his character in his *State-Worthies* (1670) when he described him as "that great Souldier and good Christian, in whom Religion was not a *softness*, (as *Machiavil* discoursed,) but a *Resolution*".[17] This combination of Machiavellian strength and religious enthusiasm he bequeathed to an heir notably hostile to all things Catholic. "But a back-friend to bishops", Arthur Grey seems to have veered towards a form of Puritanism.[18] When he was first mooted for Ireland in 1572 fears were expressed about his religious stance and its likely effect upon the political situation. In 1581 he informed Elizabeth that obedience to her warning against strictness in religious matters was, in his opinion, harmful to the government of the country.[19] His ruthless extermination of the Spanish invaders at Smerwick was partly inspired by their claim to serve the pope, their "fault" being "aggravated by the vileness of their Commander".[20] According to Camden, he demanded their unconditional surrender "inveighing very bitterly against the Bishop of Rome".[21] The author of the cautionary letter to Burghley concerning the St. Bartholomew's Day massacre could do no less. Many years later, in the aftermath of the execution of Mary Queen of Scots, Grey vigorously defended the secretary who had allegedly dispatched the death-warrant without Elizabeth's knowledge.[22] Spenser accurately portrays his attitude in *The Faerie Queene* where Artegall in "zeale of Iustice" is remorselessly "bent" upon Duessa's death (V.9.49). Grey had served as one of the Commissioners for the trial, and regarded Mary's execution as essential to the preservation of the Protestant state.

Grey's attitudes towards public life may best be gleaned from his eye-witness account of his father's campaigns in France written at the request of Raphael Holinshed. The original holograph was discovered in the mid-nineteenth century and edited for the Camden Society by a descendant of the Grey family. This document makes it clear, as Holinshed's adaptation does not, that William Grey served as the chivalric model for his son's career. Above all, Grey emphasises the special relationship between his father and the sovereign, implying, for example, that the controversial destruction of the fortifications at Chatillon in breach of an international agreement was the result of an intimate conspiracy between monarch and subject.[23] The tone of the passage makes it clear that this is precisely the sort of relationship Grey himself would have hoped to share with Elizabeth. His actual experience, chronicled in many long, frustrated letters of complaint written throughout his period as Lord Deputy, was far different.

The most interesting sections of Grey's history comprise a graphic account of the fall of Calais in 1558. Here he is at pains to portray his father, who presided over the English defeat, in the most heroic light possible, interweaving meticulously technical accounts of the siege with tales of personal derring-do, of how "jolly Mr. Gascone" was repeatedly beaten from the ramparts.[24] Most significant for our purposes, in view of his subsequent reputation in Ireland, is his attitude towards violence and compassion. The cool military professionalism which regards carnage as inevitable directly reminds one of the brusque, business-like accounts of the slaughter at Smerwick dispatched to the court in Spenser's secretary hand. Implored by the garrison at Guisnes to take pity on their lives by surrendering in the face of inevitable defeat, William Grey delivered an oration on the true nature of compassion arguing that *pity* for his comrades' honour had motivated his refusal. Had he done otherwise he might have expected his troops "to sacryfyse so hartless a captayne, rather than too take it as a toaken of a pittifull care".[25] "Wee have beegoon as beecoomed us", he continued, "lett us end then as honestie, dutie, and fame doothe wyll us". The result, not surprisingly, was mutiny. Accused of "vayne glorie", Grey was forced to compromise his principles. The victory went to the ignoble; true compassion, as the Greys understood it, was confounded in false mercy. Camden tells us that Arthur Grey wept at Smerwick and Spenser speaks of his natural tenderness, but this is not the impression one gets from the documentation.[26] Even if the details are somewhat inaccurate, the pragmatic tone of Spenser's defence of the massacre surely strikes the right note.[27] Grey refused to guarantee the lives of his enemies as a condition of their surrender, an act which was interpreted by the Spaniards themselves as sealing their doom.[28] There was nothing accidental about the subsequent butchery. Grey's conception of mercy was inextricable from his conception of duty. As his correspondence makes clear, he frequently executed prisoners and hostages as a matter of policy.[29]

The most disturbing sections of *A View* comprise Spenser's description of the Munster famine. Though often condemned out of context, this can be understood only as one intermediate stage in a well-constructed polemic designed to move towards an apparently logical conclusion. In the light of the nationwide review which constitutes the first half of his treatise, Spenser concludes that the necessary reforms can be achieved only by violent means. Since reason of state and moral duty converge we hear how "the necessity of that present state of things" forced Grey to such "violence" as the circumstances seemed to demand (*View*, p. 106). We learn of the "needful" death of "stout and obstinate rebels" (*View*, p. 103) and the "necessary" despoiling of vast tracts of territory (*View*, p. 105). Such measures it is stressed, "are not of will but of very urgent necessity" (*View*, p. 110). Encompassed within this enforced strategy is Spenser's plan for a campaign to bring Ulster to submission. In effect what he recommends is the siege of the province. Correspondences have again been found with Machiavelli, but the Italian did not invent the tactics of siege, and the strategy had frequently been employed in Ireland with varying measures of success throughout the century.[30] In order to lend weight to its present dubious viability, Spenser adduces the "profe" of the Munster famine", a direct result of Grey's policies in the early 1580s. This he describes in terrifying detail.

> Out of every corner of the woods and glens they came creeping forth upon their hands, for their legs could not bear them. They looked anatomies of death, they spake like ghosts crying out of their graves, they did eat of the dead carrions, happy were they could find them, yea and one another soon after in so much as the very carcasses they spared not to scrape out of their graves, and if they found a plot of water cress or shamrocks, there they flocked as to a feast for the time, yet not able long to continue therewithal, that in short space there were none almost left and a most populous and plentiful country suddenly left void of man or beast. yet sure in all that war there perished not many by the sword, but all by the extremity of famine, which they themselves had wrought. (*View*, p. 108).

It has been claimed that this vision filled Spenser with horror and haunted him for the rest of his life, but one must distinguish between the graphic description of something horrible in itself and a horrified account of something from which the author himself recoils.[31] The line of Spenser's argument necessitates the gruesome imagery. In political terms the image of horror is the image of success. Far from recoiling from the experience of the 1580s Spenser demands that it be repeated in the 1590s. Moreover, as Ulster is by nature less fertile than Munster, the results of a Northern famine would be proportionately worse (*View*, p. 104). Spenser is planning not merely to repeat, but to outdo, the horrors of recent history. The question of compassion he raises, and dismisses, himself:

> Therefore, by all means it must be foreseen and assured that after once entering into this course of reformation, there be afterwards no remorse or drawing back, for the sight of any such rueful object as must thereupon follow nor for compassion of their calamities, seeing that by no other means it is possible to recure them and that these are not of will, but of very urgent necessity. (*View*, p. 110)

In times of moral necessity compassion can be a vice. In *The Faerie Queene* "foolish pity" is specifically designated as one of the obstacles virtue must learn to overcome.[32] In Spenser's opinion it was Elizabeth's false sense of clemency that denied victory to Grey. No sooner had the country been "made ready for reformation" in the manner described than

> the noble Lord eftsoons was blamed, the wretched people pitied, and new counsels plotted, in which it was concluded that a general pardon should be sent over to all that would accept of it. (*View*, p. 106)

Eudoxus fears that the same may happen again:

> her sacred majesty being by nature full of mercy and clemency . . . most inclinable to such pitiful complaints . . . will not endure to hear such tragedies made of her people and poor subjects. (*View*, p. 105)

But much had changed since Grey's time. Spenser's *Legend of Justice* shows the Elizabeth of 1587 overcoming her innate sense of "piteous ruth" for the "wretched plight" of Mary Queen of Scots to sanction her execution. Significantly, he does so in the persona of Mercilla, most truly merciful when she puts the national interest before personal concerns. Formerly Parliament had deplored her "mercy" as sacrificing morality to sentiment. Her apparent change in attitude was hailed as a moral victory.[33] Spenser doubtless hoped that such new determination might also stretch to Ireland but he remains uncertain. Elizabeth publicly disavowed responsibility for Mary's death – an episode deliberately omitted from Mercilla's career – and Eudoxus fears that she may "con them litle thanks which have been the authors and counsellors of such bloody platforms" (*View*, pp. 105-6). Nevertheless, Spenser shares the pervasive view that Ireland must be won or lost within the next few years. Even at the risk of offending Elizabeth he feels impelled to move directly from a description of the famine to an uncompromising defence of the man who angered her by causing it. To exonerate Grey is to exonerate his policy. Spenser is writing not a history but a "very needful" pre-emptive tract designed to "search into the reformation of abuses" with a view to the "prevention" of "the evils to come" (*View*, p. 21). Recalling Grey from Ireland "ere he could reform it thoroughly" (V.12.27) is shown, in the course of this "search", to have been a grave error of moral and political judgement. Elizabeth is, therefore, invited to respond not emotionally, but logically, to her second, and final, chance to bring the country to heel.

The details of Spenser's defence of Grey illustrate the process whereby the historical figure became the fictional hero. As presented in *A View*, Arthur Grey has all the qualities that ensure epic stature. His dedication to the Protestant cause is unquestioned as is his willingness to implement a ruthlessly "thorough" policy. However "blotted with the name of a bloody man", he was actually "so far from delighting in blood that oftentimes he suffered not just vengeance to fall where it was deserved" (*View*, p. 106). This is not the impression created by Grey's letters but Spenser proceeds to argue for a "most gentle affable loving and temperate" nature.[34] Interestingly, however, he does admit that the "necessity" for violence "almost changed" Grey's "very natural disposition". The psychological implications of this he does not pursue nor does he entertain the possibility that Grey's initial attitude may have helped to generate the very "necessity" under which he laboured. Regrettably, the strength of Grey's convictions rendered him uniquely unsuited to his position. His was a Cromwellian dream a century before Cromwell. The very "thoroughness" of his policy eliminated the possibility of compromise and deepened native suspicions. What those suspicions were can be deduced from the wording of Grey's commission in which Elizabeth speaks of the Irish fear, "wrought in them by certayne sedetious and ill-disposed persons", that "we have a determination as it were to roote them out" and plant the entire country.[35] Grey's manner of dealing with political crises can only have exacerbated such anxieties. A Celtic observer could not but conclude that the policy of thoroughness, whatever its original intention, had come to involve the extermination of large sections of the indigenous population. This, in effect, is what happened in Munster and was now being suggested for Ulster also.

Spenser finds it easier to defend Grey within the labyrinthine allegory of *The Faerie Queene*. Graham Hough draws comfort from the fact that Talus is "an insentient robot, not a human being" symbolizing "only the swift and complete execution of the decisions that Justice has made".[36] He concludes that "there is nothing to complain of, morally or juridically, here". That so sensitive a reader should draw such a conclusion is a testament to the skilfulness of Spenser's allegorical polemic. If that allegory is to be meaningful, however, Talus must correspond to some activity in the real world where the agency is of necessity human. It is men who must become "insentient robots" if the policy of "thoroughness" is to be fully implemented. Grey was apparently prepared to make such a sacrifice "almost" to the "changing" of his "very natural disposition". In a tract intended for a select, private audience, Spenser can make admissions inappropriate to a great national epic.

In *The Faerie Queene* Spenser proceeds by making a series of crucial allegorical distinctions or "detachments" designed to further his personal interpretation of Irish history. In the first place he adroitly detaches "Ireland" from the native Irish. As a result, Irena's real identity becomes rather problematic. Her role in the romance narrative is to beseech and obtain Gloriana's aid against the injustice of Grandtorto. In dispatching Artegall to "worke *Irenae's* franchisement" (V.11.36), Gloriana becomes the compassionate "Patronesse" of "weake Princes" (V.1.4) apparently disinterested in her act of intervention. Spenser, too, felt a "greate Compassion" for a "moste beautiful and sweet country" utterly "wasted and left desolate" by the events of recent history – the desolation wrought by Lord Grey being of a different moral order (*View*, pp. 18-19). Thus compassion for the "country" emerges as a moral and political virtue whereas compassion for the indigenous population is identified as moral and political vice. The crowds of people who rejoice at the death of Grandtorto, "glad to quit from that proud Tyrant's awe" are not, as Elizabethan readers are led to imagine, the native Irish. No sooner has the giant fallen than they rush to proclaim Irena "their true Liege and Princesse naturall" (V.12.24). But Spenser is committed to the view that there is no Irish sovereignty independent of the English crown. Consequently the country can have but one "true Liege and Princesse naturall" and Irena, by a highly solipsistic inversion, proves to be a pseudonym of Gloriana. In dispatching Artegall to Irena's aid, Gloriana defends her own "weake" cause by ensuring the elimination of all "lewd disposed traitors that shall dare lift up their heel against their sovereign lady" [herself]" (*View*, p. 96). One remembers how at the outset of Artegall's quest, Irena blossoms "like as a tender Rose in open plaine" (V.12.13). The imagery is borrowed from Ariosto, but in retrospect one realises that Artegall's approach to Ireland serves primarily to cultivate the Tudor rose.[37]

Having successfully dissociated Ireland from the Irish people, Spenser proceeds to dissociate the country's evils from those who perpetrate them. According to his definition of the royal "sword" the object of justified violence is the eradication of evil itself not evil people, "for evil people by good ordinance and government may be made good, but the evil that is of itself evil will never become good" (*View*, p. 77). In practice, of course, Grey found it impossible to maintain such a distinction and only a few paragraphs later we hear of the need to destroy "all that rebellious rout of loose *people*" who oppose the Elizabethan regime (*View*, p. 95). It may well have been that Spenser wished to distinguish "grand" rebels from their humbler followers (although "rout" can scarcely bear such an interpretation) or represent Grey's role as rescuing the "mere" Irish from the tyranny of old Norman families such as the Desmonds – contemporary annotations to Book Five indicate that Grandtorto was occasionally identified with various members of the Desmond family.[38] Neither distinction sorts well with recorded history. Grey actively opposed Elizabeth's practice of granting pardons in the hope of reconciling former opponents to her cause and Spenser presumably agreed with his patron. In any case the reader of *The Faerie Queene* is inured to the slaughter of "evil" people by a number of rhetorical devices: The victims are invariably dehumanised into an amorphous "rout" so that there is no recognisable individual with whom one can sympathise. Similarly the imagery is designed to concentrate attention upon the activity rather than the recipients. Talus's flail merely winnows unwonted chaff (V.1.127) or fells malefactors "as thicke as . . . seede after the sowers hand" (V.12.7). In this instance ferocious violence is sublimated into an image of revitalisation: it is difficult to remember that the "seeds" are corpses, the furrows mass graves.

Just as the common people are presented as a "rout", so their leaders are metamorphosed into monsters, dragons, and giants. The allegorical interpretation of the resulting combats transforms Grey's blood victories into conceptual victories. The reader is thus constantly led away from the human implications of the policy of "thoroughness". Yet perhaps the most successful "detachment" of all is that noticed, and appreciated, by Graham Hough: the dissociation of Lord Grey from his own brutality.[39] In the world of the poem's moral heroism necessary violence cannot be allowed to all but subvert the hero's "very natural disposition" towards compassion. Another character must be created to bear the burden of blood-guilt and that character is Talus, an iron-man or machine incapable of self-recrimination. Throughout the poem Artegall is represented as *restraining* Talus who frequently begins to act quite independently of his lord. This aspect of Artegall's role is particularly emphasised in the Irena passages where, having checked Talus, he asserts that, "not for such slaughters sake/He thether came, but for to trie the right/Of fayre *Irenaes* cause with him in single fight" (V.12.8). Fiction here takes complete leave of historical reality. We are invited to understand the episode in strictly conceptual terms as a conflict between justice and tort, a conflict without "slaughter". Artegall emerges as a paragon of chivalric courage and his defeat of Grandtorto falls naturally into the pattern of all similar heroic combats described in the preceding four books. One hardly notices how, after the fall of Grandtorto, Talus is freed to deal with "all such persons, as did late maintayne/That tyrants part". So effective is he that "in short space . . . not one was left" who dares disobey Irena (V.12.25). The line is ambiguous. Does it mean that they are all dead or merely all obedient? "Not one was left" is ominous. One recalls the account of the Munster famine: "in short space there were none almost left and a most populous and plentiful country suddenly left void of man or beast" (*View*, p. 104). The dissociation of Ireland from the Irish is complete.

Grey failed in his attempt to "reform" Ireland but that failure is attributed both in *A View* and *The Faerie Queene* to the malice of powerful enemies at court.[41] In the poem these enemies are transformed into the loathsome personifications of Envie and Detraction. With the result that the charges levelled against Grey are discredited in their very uttrance (V.12.40).[41] As Artegall restrains Talus for the last time the reader is invited to applaud a familiar moral response (V.12.43) but in terms of the historical allegory the action is meaningless since Grey could not unleash against Elizabeth's political advisers the forces Talus represents. To decipher the episode in this manner is, of course, to break the poetic spell but historical allegory invites historical interpretation. To the extent that writers such as Spenser allegorise not history but a personal vision of history their works involve an element of wish-fulfilment if not self-delusion. The real world remains tantalizingly out of phase with its fictional counterpart and the resulting tension disturbs the balance of the poetry. Since it can offer no moral reason for Artegall's disappointment, Spenser's narrative must content itself with political satire. Spenser believed in Arthur Grey and it is faith not historical accuracy that his allegory reflects.

The central flaw of the *Legend of Justice* has long been regarded as its confusion of moral and political values, its defence of the indefensible. Such confusion is the inevitable consequence of religious nationalism, of equating the fate of the nation with that of the chosen race. The Old Testament records centuries of equally bloody, equally lauded, ruthlessness. In his "Letter to Raleigh" Spenser distinguishes between ethics, the code of private morality, and politics, the code of government. He implies, however, that politics depend upon ethics and finds in the person of Virgil's Aeneas the pattern of both.[42] Prince Arthur must show himself a "vertuous man" before he may become a "good governour". Private morality develops into public policy. Thus, in the Protestant cause, Spenser can reconcile moral necessity to political necessity, providential historiography to reason of state. It is a reconciliation calculated to appeal only to like-minded theorists. Celtic poets also developed concepts of moral and national heroism in many respects similar to Spenser's own. The crucial difference was that of political allegiance. Spenser praises their poetic style while deploring their subject-matter as "licentious", employing this term in a political rather than a sexual sense. The heroism of which they approve tends "to the hurt of the English or maintenance of their own lewd liberty" (*View*, p. 74). In this way the concept of political liberty is confounded in that of moral libertinism.[43] Confronted by the mirror image of himself – poets who espouse violent methods in the cause of Celtic independence and Catholicism – Spenser finds the spectacle morally degrading. No ripple of conscious irony disturbs the flow of his prose: the Protestant establishment has been identified with the moral order and all who oppose it "receive unto themselves damnation".

1. For Spenser's use of Machiavelli see Edwin A. Greenlaw, "The Influence of Machiavelli on Spenser", *Modern Philology* 7 (1909), 187-202; H. S. V. Jones, "Spenser's Defence of Lord Grey", *University of Illinois Studies in Language and Literature* 5 (1919), 151-219.
2. *A Preface to "The Faerie Queene"* (London, 1962), pp. 195, 196, 198.
3. *The Discourses* (II.33), tr. Leslie J. Walker, ed. Bernard Crick (Harmondsworth, 1970), pp. 381-2.
4. *The Prince*, tr. and ed. George Bull (Harmondsworth, 1961), pp. 36, 48. See also pp. 57-8.
5. Quentin Skinner, *The Foundation of Modern Political Thought* (Cambridge, 1978), Vol. I, pp. 250-1.
6. Skinner, pp. 251-4.
7. *City of God*, XIX, 7. See also Aquinas, *Summa Theologica*, II, ii, q. 40.
8. Maurice Keen, *Chivalry* (London, 1984), pp. 49-50.
9. John Erskine Hankins, *Source and Meaning in Spenser's Allegory* (Oxford, 1971), pp. 99-119.
10. Arthur B. Ferguson, *Clio Unbound: Perception of the Social and Cultural Past in Renaissance England* (Durham, North Carolina, 1979), p. 381.
11. *A Commentary of the Services and Charges of William Lord Grey of Wilton . . . by Arthur Lord Grey of Wilton*, ed. Sir Philip de Malpas Grey Egerton, Camden Society (London, 1847), p. 70. Hereafter Grey.
12. *A Collection of State Papers . . . for the Year 1571-96*, ed. William Murdin (London, 1759), pp. 356-7. Hereafter Murdin.
13. For Grey's fear of invasion see Murdin, p. 347. See also *Calendar of State Papers (Irish) 1574-85*, p. 267.
14. Grey, p. 66.
15. *View*, p. 95; Murdin, p. 354; *The Life and Correspondence of Lodowick Bryskett*, ed. Henry R. Plomer and Tom Peete Cross (Chicago, 1927), pp. 23, 31. Hereafter Bryskett.
16. According to William Camden, Perrot "did very good Service, though he were now and then blamed by the *English*, as too favourable to the Irish, and too rigid to the *English*. But he, by administering Justice indifferently, and shewing equall Favour to the *Irish* and the *English*, restored the Countrey by little and little to a welcome Tranquillity". *The History of Princess Elizabeth* (London, 1675), p. 291. Hereafter Camden.
17. (London, 1670), p. 571.
18. "In all Divisions of Votes in Parliament or Council-Table, [he] sided with the Antiprelatial party." *State-Worthies*, p. 589.
19. *Calendar of State Papers (Irish) 1574-85*, p. 275.
20. *The Works of Edmund Spenser: A Variorum Edition*, ed. E. Greenlaw, C. G. Osgood, F. M. Padelford, Vol. X: The Prose Works (Baltimore, 1949), Appendix II, p. 524. Hereafter *Prose*. For Grey's attitude to Ireland see Raymond Jenkins, "Spenser with Lord Grey in Ireland", *Publications of the Modern Language Association* 52 (1937), 338-53.
21. Camden, p. 243.
22. Camden, pp. 391-2. Rather incongruously, Grey had been accused in earlier years of sympathy for Mary. See *The Works of Edmund Spenser: A Variorum Edition*, Vol. V:

The Faerie Queene, Book V (1936). His speech intentionally dispels any lingering suspicion.

23. Grey, pp. 5-9.
24. Grey, p. 20.
25. Grey, pp. 35-6.
26. Camden, p. 243; *View*, p. 106.
27. Grey can dismiss the execution of hostages with the phrase, "I committed to Justice his first Pledges", Murdin, p. 362. Spenser concludes of the executions at Smerwick, "there was no other way but to make that short end of them which was made" (*View*, p. 108).
28. *Prose*, p. 526.
29. Murdin, pp. 348, 356, 362.
30. Rudolf Gottfried recalls *The Arte of Warre*, "it is better to conquere the enemie with famine, than with yron" (*Prose*, p. 377).
31. M. M. Gray, "The Influence of Spenser's Irish Experiences on *The Faerie Queene*", *Review of English Studies* 6 (1930), 413-28 (p. 424).
32. See, for example, II.12.29 and V.5.13-16.
33. Rene Graziani, "Elizabeth at Isis Church", *Publications of the Modern Language Association* 79 (1964), 376-89 (pp. 279-80).
34. Gray's allusions to his own gentle spirit (*Prose*, p. 384) are completely undercut by his explanations of policy: "I take no Delight to advertise of every common Persons head that is taken of. Otherwise I could have certified of an Hundredth or two of their lives ended since my coming from these Parts" (Murdin, p. 347).
35. Grey, p. 75.
36. Hough, p. 196. For a less indulgent view see Michael O'Connell, *Mirror and Veil: The Historic Dimension of Spenser's "Faerie Queene"* (Chapel Hill, North Carolina, 1977), pp. 156-9.
37. *Orlando Furioso*, XXXII.108. See "E.K."'s note to *The Shepheardes Calender*, "April", l. 68.
38. Anon., "MSS. Notes to Spenser's *Faerie Queene*", *Notes and Queries* 202 (1957), 509-15 (p. 513).
39. Hough, p. 196.
40. Spenser suppresses the fact that Grey in desperation urged his own recall. Grey, p. 79.
41. "Most untruly and maliciously do these evil tongues backbite and slander the sacred ashes of that most just and honourable personage" (*View*, p. 108). According to Bryskett, "envie it self cannot touche" Grey's "sinceritie" (Bryskett, p. 39).
42. Smith and de Selincourt, p. 407.
43. Grey, too, deplored Elizabeth's apparent decision to allow the Irish "wallow in their own sensual government" (Jenkins, p. 345).

Index